IT GETS ME HOME,

THIS CURVING TRACK

Ian Penman is a British writer, music journalist, and critic. He began his career at the *NME* in 1977, later contributing to various publications including *The Face*, *Arena*, *Tatler*, *Uncut*, *Sight & Sound*, *The Wire*, the *Guardian*, the *LRB*, and *City Journal*. He is the author of *Vital Signs: Music, Movies, and Other Manias* (Serpent's Tail, 1998).

'Ian Penman is an ideal critic, one who invites you in, takes your coat, and hands you a drink as he sidles up to his topic. He has a modest mien, a feathery way with a sentence, a century's worth of adroit cultural connections at the ready, and a great well of genuine passion, which quickly raises the temperature. Penman writes about the monuments of popular music as if he had a personal stake in them – which of course he does.'
—— Luc Sante, author of *The Other Paris*

'Writing about music can often be a joyless and rather sterile exercise in point-scoring, fact-shaming and imposition of the party line, but rather than engage in musical vivisection, Ian Penman's mercurial, teasing, provocative prose presents him as a tap dancer – one who happens to use his fingers instead of his feet, and a keyboard instead of a sprung floor. Whether you agree with everything he says is beside the point. What matters is that he aspires to make the same shapes and rhythms on paper as his subjects do with particles of air.'
—— Will Ashon, author of *Chamber Music*

'Ian Penman – critic, essayist, mystical hack and charmer of sentences like they're snakes – is the writer I have hardly gone a week without reading, reciting, summoning to mind. The writer *without whom*, etc. ... I was 15 when I first read Penman, and practically all I thought about was music. After Penman, I thought about language, too. About the ways a young life might be diverted by the wrong words, the wrong metaphors – how you might find the right ones in a stray song lyric or the corner of a magazine page. ... The writing is frequently something entirely else: decades of love and listening translated into prose that glides and shimmies and pivots on risky metaphors, low puns, highbrow reference points. ... I wouldn't have written a word without the dream, ghost, echo of his writing.'
—— Brian Dillon, *frieze*

'Ian Penman is popular music's Hazlitt – its chief stylist – and his sound is often equal to what he writes about. Each of his essays is an event, so this book is indispensable.'
—— Andrew O'Hagan, author of *The Secret Life*

'Written with love and joy and squirt gunner's accuracy with the adjective.'
—— Nicholson Baker, author of *U & I*

'A laureate of marginal places.'
—— Iain Sinclair, *London Review of Books*

Fitzcarraldo Editions

IT GETS ME HOME,
THIS CURVING TRACK

IAN PENMAN

MIHI CIVITATEM
... all the black & white cats.

CONTENTS

INTRODUCTION [15]

EVEN IF YOU HAVE TO STARVE: THE
LONG HORIZONS OF MOD [24]

DID HE FEEL GOOD? JAMES BROWN'S
EPIC LIFE AND CAREER [40]

BIRDITIS: THE OBSESSION WITH
CHARLIE PARKER [56]

SWOONATRA: THE AFTERLIVES
OF FRANK SINATRA [76]

THE FAST BIRTH AND SLOW DEATH OF
ELVIS AARON PRESLEY [98]

HALF IN LOVE WITH BLIND JOE DEATH:
GUITAR VIRTUOSO JOHN FAHEY'S
AMERICAN ODYSSEY 115

SO HIP IT HURTS: STEELY DAN'S
DONALD FAGEN LOOKS BACK 128

THE QUESTION OF U: THE MIRROR
IMAGE OF PRINCE 146

INTRODUCTION

'Isn't this musicality, which seems suddenly to be exhaled by things, so that it brings them into tune with me, the symbol of what I have desired for a long time: no longer to be in the position of a stranger in a world where I alternately doze off and stir myself in pointless agitation?'
—— Michel Leiris, *The Trumpet-Drum*

If I told you 'It gets me home / this curving track...' is a line I stole from a thirteenth-century Sufi poem, or a nineteenth-century British folk song, or a 1930s Deep South blues holler, would you believe me? It's actually taken from the 1958 W. H. Auden poem 'Walks', but when I came across it one blurry insomniac morning it seemed to leap off the pristine Faber & Faber page – a lovely description of spinning vinyl, and also words that might have sprung from any number of unkempt and long-favoured songs. I can imagine this line being sung by The Carter Family say, or Skip James and Shirley Collins or Van Morrison or Taj Mahal, or maybe even in one of those slow, strange, melancholy tracks that Underworld sometimes do. In my mind's ear I can hear it issuing forth from Kate Bush, or buried away in the echoic waveforms of a new Burial mix. It could be a lost album of pastoral keening by the late and sorely missed Coil. It could be the title of a book by Charles Bukowski in his 60s/70s prime, to fit alongside all-time favourites such as *It Catches My Heart in Its Hands* or *The Days Run Away Like Wild Horses Over The Hills* or (wait for it) *Play the Piano Drunk Like a Percussion Instrument Until the Fingers Begin to Bleed a Bit*. It could be the one phrase you clearly understood on a page by Heidegger...

Another couplet from the same Auden poem: 'The repetition it involves / Raises a doubt it never solves.' This also seems to me to suggest some of the strange pull and operation of certain hypnotic musics. Another couplet from a different poet: 'How does it feel / To be without a home?' The irony here is that when Dylan flung out such biting lines in the mid-60s, they made a lot of people feel – in some cases, for the very first time – a little less lonely, mapless, passed over. When all else fails, when our compass is broken, there is one thing some of us have come to rely on: music really can give us a sense of something like home. Just in the last few hours' work, my background music, more or less at random, included: Carmen McRae singing Lennon and McCartney's 'Carry That Weight': 'Once there was a way / to get back homeward...' Gram Parsons and The Flying Burrito Brothers: 'Won't you sing me back home ... with a song I used to hear.' Bob Neuwirth: 'Far from home, every late night two-bit jukebox / Has a song for someone that's gone.' Johnny Thunders: 'And when I'm home / big deal... I'm still alone.' Steely Dan: 'Could it be that I have found my home at last? / Home at last.' And finally, definitively, Jane's Addiction and an oddly hypnotic one-word song: 'Home... home...' How to build a home or community and how to do so in a time of increasing fragmentation, and what meanings we might find (or re-find) there – these are matters that never grow old or stale. There's a line in the film *Cutter's Way* which always gets me (though perhaps not so much now as it did a few decades back, when I was simultaneously resistant to the idea of home, and secretly desperate for one), when Mo says to the blithe hedonist Bone: 'Is it so bad to have somewhere to come home to, Richie, when you got nowhere else to go?' Partly, of course, it's how the actress Lisa Eichorn delivers this line – the music her voice makes of it. *Cutter's Way* could be seen as a meditation on how dissimilar people made unlikely homes or families for themselves in very un-straightforward ways, at a time in America when a lot of wounded boys/men, black and white, came back 'home' from an obscenely pointless war. (For more on this, I recommend the Kent CD, *A Soldier's Sad Story: Vietnam Through The Eyes of Black America 1966-73*.)

This is now the sixth or seventh introduction I've attempted. Some of the other versions had thousands of words about my past and what was there that fed into these essays, indeed, into wanting to write about music at all. I decided any such contextual backdrop was not only unnecessary, but perhaps contra what I felt was the whole spirit of the thing. I might say that my own life has been one lived without a hometown, or even a definite accent or nationality, and that such an unstable background doubtless shaped my own feelings about ideas of home. I might also say that the current ideal I have for my own work is a kind of writing that is entirely accessible to whomsoever might happen by; but one that also repays repeated readings, if these occur. In other words: anyone can dip in and out of the text... but at the same time, there may be a web of half-hidden clues, suggestions, portents insinuated between or behind the lines, there for you to find. If you catch them – great; if you don't, that's also just fine. I do have to admit, re-reading some of these pieces again for the book I was surprised by how much of my life I occasionally let slip. What you don't want in a book of collected essays is stuff that relies too much on now disappeared topicality, on passing context. As it goes, some of my own favourite books – books I've read and re-read many times – are collections of reviews or journalism. To the left of the keyboard I'm writing this on, there is a whole wall of books that is entirely non-fiction; earlier this morning I happened to pluck out a collection by the Anglo-Irish writer Hubert Butler (a self-described 'Protestant Republican'), whose essays straddle a somewhat risky boundary line – on one side a deep love of home, and purely local resonance; on the other, an equal need to venture out into a world of sometimes frightening difference.

If there's anything that connects the younger, more reckless, more combative (OK: self-centred) me, and today's I-would-hope more reflective, less tricksy self, it's probably the search for a certain tone in writing – how to be serious without being pompous, how to be simultaneously complex and seductive, how to give a hint of your own flaws and passions without being boorishly or presumptively autobiographical. I find that tone in some of the music that is considered here – Bill Evans, Frank Sinatra, Donald Fagen – in how it manages to be instantly, charmingly accessible, but with repeated plays you realize it also contains all kinds of winks and twists and undertones. Something else that links some of the subjects of some of these essays is a certain taut dialectic between a messy and even desperate private life and the artist's almost supernaturally elegant, economical song. (This is also true of certain writers I love: John Cheever, Jean Rhys, Joseph Roth.) If you pushed me, I might even suggest there was almost a kind of 'politics' in such economy. Of course, the other side of this – which I brush against in the John Fahey piece – is how much moral latitude we're prepared to allow such artists in their private lives before we say 'Enough'. How much egregiously bad behaviour we're prepared to put up with or overlook or excuse for the chance of great, even redemptive art.

In Robert Gordon's marvellous book *It Came From Memphis*, I found this quote from the songwriter, producer and session musician Dan Penn: 'In terms of the races, the 60s was the culmination of the 40s and 50s. There was a lot of white people and black people who had tried to bring the R&B and the white side together. It became a white/black situation, you had white players and black players together. The mixture, who knows what that does to us, but it does something.'

And who knows what it does to you when you are a shy and gawky, unformed and insecure 14-year-old, in flattest dullest 1970s Norfolk? As it happens, another way of expressing Penn's thought crops up in a 1941 piece by Hubert Butler, called 'The Barriers', where he writes: 'Great cultures have always risen from the interaction of diverse societies. And where that interaction has been varied, easy and reciprocated ... national genius has expressed itself most freely.'

Something else Penn goes on to say: 'I always related a record to painting a picture. Your speakers, or one speaker back then, you stretch this big old canvas – I see it, I try to physically see it. That cross-colour respect was a wonderful thing.' Is it intentional what Penn does there – that subtle echoing repetition or modulation of the phrase 'cross-colour'? Which, in a certain way, is the whole seed of this book. When I was fourteen I was obsessed with two things: drawing/painting and soul music. Indeed, I was all set on going to art school eventually, and had no real thought of writing at all, never mind for a living, or a lifetime. But then – but then, that is a tale for another book. Much as I loved the social aspect of punk, the music didn't quite do it for me (although

I've recently been having something like a second adolescence, re-discovering a lot of that same 70s rock); perhaps one reason was that I'd already had a form of punk revelation through certain wild R&B from the likes of Swamp Dogg (*Total Destruction To Your Mind*!), Funkadelic (*Maggot Brain*!), or Howlin' Wolf (the sheer screechy lo-fi car-smash aesthetic of Hubert Sumlin's guitar in 'How Many More Years'!). It wasn't a matter of a smart lyric or a technically impressive guitar solo – it was the sound, the sonics, the tone. It was blues but it wasn't raggedy and depressed. It was soul but it wasn't smooth and sultry – it was some kind of a self-dislocating mind-sparking soul-sluicing apocalypse.

Again, Dan Penn sums it all up in a few words, talking about how when he was younger, Bobby Bland or Aretha Franklin completely sent him in a way the rock-and-roll(i)er Chuck Berry never did: 'He was cute and he was smart, but he never went to church. I never heard that in his voice.' *He never went to church.* I don't think Penn means it in a literal sense (though this can apply: see the Elvis and James Brown pieces here), but somewhere altogether elsewhere and unexpected the music takes you, somewhere that's hard to name. If you don't already know *It Came From Memphis* I do recommend you find a copy (ditto Peter Guralnick's *Sweet Soul Music*, Dr John's *Under A Hoodoo Moon* and Stanley Booth's *Rythm Oil*). Thinking back, it seems to me no coincidence that among the tsunami of recent music books, the ones I found most surprising (and surprisingly paradigm-warping) have all been reassessments in one way or another of the early Blues culture. (Examples: Stephen Calt's *I'd Rather Be The Devil: Skip James and the Blues*; Nick Tosches' *Where Dead Voices Gather*; Elijah Wald's *Escaping The Delta*.)

If there's a kind of buried or half-obscured alchemical emblem behind *It Gets Me Home*..., it's the image of Dan Penn & Spooner Oldham, two skinny white boys huddled together in a small-town diner, writing songs like 'Do Right Woman' and 'Dark End of The Street'. Penn & Oldham, along with contemporaries such as Jim Dickinson and Chips Moman, and all of their fellow musicians in the Dixie Flyers and Muscle Shoals studio bands – I didn't know it at the time, but a lot of the soul/R&B records I loved as a teenager that completely turned my head around had these characters' fingerprints all over them. Here is a last quote from *It Came From Memphis* about Atlantic producer Tom Dowd: 'I walk in one day and [he] is talking to Dusty Springfield, who is musically educated. He's talking pianissimo and obligato, and the next day I walk in and he's in there passing a bucket of chicken round with Joe Tex.'

Without getting too misty eyed about all this, it seems to me there is a whole vanished world summed up here. A moment... the collision or commingling of two cultures... the birth of a certain kind of cross-generational and 'cross-colour' awareness. We can argue about what precisely led up to this, and what happened afterwards or didn't, but undeniably – there was that moment, and it was glorious. Just go and play some Aretha and you'll hear its echoes – palpable, wilful, beguiling.

Which brings us neatly to something of an embarrassed admission.

There is an empty chair at the centre of this book, and in an ideal world it would be occupied by Billie Holiday. She's been a central and recurring and catalytic presence in my emotional/critical life, and I can feel her shadowy outline behind a lot of the writing here. I was offered a chance to review the most recent Billie biography, John Szwed's excellent *Billie Holiday: The Musician & The Myth*, for the books pages of *The Wire*; but in words all too apt for a long-time Billie-phile, I just couldn't get started. Or, to be more accurate, I couldn't get started with the idea in back of my mind that I'd have to draw things to some kind of conclusion in a mere (!) 900 words or so. (Being allowed to work out your thoughts at some length for a publication like the *LRB* can perhaps spoil you, in certain ways, for other more deadline-intensive work.) I do have years', no, decades' worth of writing on Billie Holiday, for a long planned book (variously titled, down the years: *Cuts, Tracks & Bruises – The Weakening Beat – Little White Flowers*) which hopefully will finally see the light of day quite soon, and make up for this omission. It would also have been great if I could have written about two more recent passions – Solange Knowles and Lana Del Rey. Both would have fitted the underlying schematic of this collection, but it was not to be – the reviewer-essayist is more often than not a kind of a literary cabby, waiting to be hailed and told where to go.

I do wonder if I might not have been happier with Solange or even her big sister closing this collection – and hinting at certain futures - than what turned out to be a very long and oddly dispiriting goodbye to Prince. There have been biographies of other artists I love – Borges, Van Morrison, Harry Crews – that I've regretted reading, either because it made them too dully, fallibly human, or distracted too radically from the long-adored work, or because they simply weren't up to the multi-hued complexity of the artist in question. But three years and a lot of reading on from his death, I still have the uncanny, and slightly unpleasant feeling of being not an inch nearer any deeper 'understanding' of Prince. As if there was the man and there was some kind of rigorously controlled image, and in-between ... nothing. You reach out for him and come away with air, or handfuls of fake fur; and the bits that do seem a tiny bit clearer turn out to be far from pleasant.

And just as I was in the home straitght of finishing up *It Gets Me Home*..., Solange announced the release of her latest album. And what was it called...? *When I Get Home*. Big smile. CUT.

IP, 31/3/19, TO THE BACKGROUND MUSIC OF BETTY LAVETTE: CHILD OF THE 70S.

EVEN IF YOU HAVE TO STARVE:
THE LONG HORIZONS OF MOD

In a lovely 1963 piece on Miles Davis, Kenneth Tynan quotes Cocteau to illuminate the art of his 'discreet, elliptical' subject: Davis was one of those twenti-eth-century artists who had found 'a simple way of saying very complicated things'. Jump to 1966 and the meatier, beatier sound of a UK Top 20 hit, the Who's 'Substitute', a vexed, stuttering anti-manifesto, with its self-accusatory boast: 'The simple things you see are all complicated!' You couldn't find two more different mu-sical cries: Davis's liquid tone is hurt, steely, recessive, where Townshend's is upfront, impatient, hectoring. One arrow points in, the other out. But somewhere in the journey from one to the other, from cool, cruel blue to Townshend's three-minute psychodrama – 'I look all white / but my dad was black' – was the brief, paradoxi-cal flare of Mod: the story of how a small cabal of British jazz obsessives conducting a besotted affair with the style arcana of Europe and America somehow became an army of scooter-borne rock fans, draped in the am-biguous insignia of RAF targets and Union Jacks.

What Richard Weight calls the 'very British style' of Mod found its initial foothold in late 1950s Soho with the arrival of the jazz 'modernists', who defined themselves in strict opposition to the reigning gatekeepers of Trad. Modernists were wilfully brittle, stylish, working-class Cains, different in every way from the whoop-it-up trad jazz Abels. Trad – hugely and improbably popular in its day – had a predominantly middle to upper-class and purposively vulgar fanbase. In its ranks were Kingsley Amis, Philip Larkin and George Melly, who all later wrote of this time as of a lost Eden. Larkin's jazz column for the *Telegraph* ran from 1961 to 1968, a period roughly coextensive with Mod's quiet rise and noisy fall.

Trads embraced a louche, boho scruffiness (silly hats, sloppy jumpers, duffle coats), where Mods dressed with considered exactness. Trads were British to a fault (real ale, CND, the Goons) while the Mods had a magpie eye for European style, from the Tour de France to the Nouvelle Vague. Trads followed Acker Bilk, Mods worshipped Thelonious Monk: even at fifty years' remove, you can see how sharing the same club, city or country might have been problematic. If the Oxbridgey Trads had a philosophical pin-up it was Bertrand Russell, with Freddie Ayer for real deep kicks; Mods backed the darker horse of existentialism. How much the Mod crush on continental philosophy was a pose, and how much serious engagement, is a moot point. Even as 'mere' pose it's a very interesting one. In the dourly socialist cinema of the British New Wave, working-class characters are portrayed as sooty beasts of burden, life-force bruisers, twelve pints a night men; Camus-rifling aesthetes are thin on the cobbled ground.

Trad appealed to folk who were more or less content with the way things were along a certain squeaky corridor of Englishness. Mods felt an obscure pinch of agita at the thought of what their future promised. American jazz and European movies weren't just crib sheets for how to wear loafers and a cravat, they were permission slips that allowed their audiences to pause and reflect. Trad reactionaries and Mod wideboys? Doubtless it was never quite so cut and dried. Skim the sub rosa lit of the time (Robin Cook, Alexander Baron, Colin MacInnes) and you're plunged into a lost river with discrete but commingled tributaries: gay, criminal, East End Jewish, upper-class drop-out, lower-class dandy; the 'morries' of Cook's dodgy Chelsea set, and Baron's Harryboy Boas, a proto-Mod. 'One thing about me, I always dress smartly,' Boas declares. 'A good suit, midnight blue mohair, this year's cut. Dazzling white shirt, quiet tie of silk, rust-colour. Buy your clothes good if you have to starve afterwards.'

Weight devotes as little space to the early 'modernist' period as he can get away with. Movements of thought are, admittedly, harder to track than fashionable hemlines, but he seems palpably incurious about this smudgy horizon. Sartre gets a single sentence referencing his 'famous dictum that "One must act to be free."' Hang about – is that his famous dictum? I'm a bit hazy after forty years, but off the top of my head (current haircut modelled after the sleeve of *Chet Baker & Crew*, Pacific Records, 1956) wasn't it 'Existence precedes essence'? Or: 'Man is condemned to be free'? Or (surely a contender for a TV quiz show clincher): 'Hell is ... other people!'? I fed the 'famous dictum' into Google and it was nowhere to be found (Weight supplies no attribution). Existentialism likewise gets a single ... oh, wait, it's the same sentence as Sartre. They share a sentence. Halvsies. (You'd think Weight might at least have mentioned Sartre's Mod-like appetite for amphetamines; if ever a novel read like one long comedown from a teeth-grinding high, it's *Nausea*.)

Further down the road, Mod became more about buying the right records and wearing the approved uniform, but in the nervy modernist dawn there was a real hunger for films, books, dialogue; or as Weight puts it in the first subheading of his introduction: 'Amphetamines, Jean-Paul Sartre and John Lee Hooker'. Which is a nice phrase, even if it's half-inched from an interviewee in a previous book, Jonathon Green's flawless oral history of

1960s counterculture, *Days in the Life*. (In fact Green also used it as a subheading. This feels a bit previous to me: to use someone else's quote OK, but their layout too?) The early Mods were navigators, Magellans of the postwar field of leisure time, which had to be imagined, cast in this or that shape. Everything was up for grabs: music and clothes, sex and sexuality; the speech and language of put-down and put-on and pop fandom; transport and travel; nights out and nights in. Everything, in fact, we now take for granted as 'youth culture'. It was a heady time of redefinition; but we also get the first migraine flash of a paradox that would split Mod, and define other subcultures: what began as a principled refusal of the nine-to-five wage-slave grind found its most vivid street-level expression in avid consumerism. As Peter Gay put it, paraphrasing Walter Gropius: 'The cure for the ills of modernity is more, and the right kind, of modernity.' This could be Mod speaking.

Gay's reflection is from his 1968 book *Weimar Culture*, and its subtitle is also applicable here: *The Outsider as Insider*. The tension between wanting to be unique but needing to belong underlies all subcultures. For the Mods, as with the Situationists (awol from Weight's index), there was a conflict between rowdy group identity and individual slant. They mixed outdoor jaunt with indoor dissipation, group jamboree with sombre reflection, and they took very small things very seriously indeed, things other people wrongly perceived as frivolous. The Mod obsession with Blue Note album sleeves and Italian fashion had the quality of fetish, in both the Marxist and ritual senses. It required near-fanatical commitment to 'source' the materials required for a makeover. (In the early 1970s when I was a teenager, the high street was still hopeless, a fashion desert: *Are You Being Served?* was as much social realism as ribald sitcom.) Early Mod shared with Bauhaus an almost puritan obsession with clean style and correct design. Early Mods had a deserved rep for sartorial aloofness, which shaded into a kind of radiant anonymity. Like the 'man of the crowd' in Baudelaire (and Benjamin) they were in the crowd but not of it, tracking sociability like spooks instead of being haplessly caught up in it like everyone else.

Early Mods could 'pass' between work and play without changing their suits, which is perhaps one of the reasons they were never sent up in the culture at large. Think back to 1960s and 1970s low comedy: no TV sketch show or sitcom or kitschy horror film was complete without its parade of subcult Aunt Sallies – hippies, ton-up boys, skinheads, punks. Rockers had shivs, skinheads had bovver boots, hippies might dose you – what was a Mod going to do? Make you listen to Otis Redding? Force you to buy a decent pair of trousers? Mods posed a far less obvious threat. They flew the Union Jack, after all, and most of them had jobs; they were clean, well turned-out and had nice haircuts. In 1964 there was a brief spasm of tabloid outrage over some rather tame skirmishes between Mods and Rockers, mostly conducted in bracing seaside ozone. Talk of scooter-borne 'vermin' aside, the real fear may have had less to do with physical aggro and more to do with the difficulty of slotting Mod into any obvious class or subcult genealogy. (Even the word 'subculture' suggests soil, shadow, dirt; airless oubliettes; greasy rungs leading down into a Harry Lime exile.)

Class plays through this story in sighing counterpoint, but Weight has the pop sociological equivalent of a tin ear. He relies entirely on secondary research, on other people's now exaggerated accounts of already faded memories, and has zero feeling for real lives, real voices, real flight and fall. There is a dusty old pub-table anecdote about some Mod who would only have bunk-up sex if there was a trouser press to hand for his strides – which is presumably meant as a dig at Mod's twisted priorities. (Full disclosure: no trouser press, but I do own two pairs of antique shoe trees.) Another way to see this tale: having saved for months to afford a gorgeous suit, and probably unable to afford a replacement any time soon, you're going to make damned sure it lasts. Maybe this guy was on a 48-hour weekender and didn't want to roll into work on Monday morning looking like an undignified mess?

Still, Weight's basic thesis seems unexceptionable: Mod as the beginning of everything we now take for granted in style culture, the 'DNA of British youth culture, leaving its mark on glam and Northern Soul, punk and Two Tone, Britpop and rave'. But DNA is one thing, 'leaving a mark' quite another. Was Mod central and catalytic, or peripheral and intermittent? Because Mod itself came to signify so many different things to so many different people, and because Weight fails to separate out and clearly define words like 'dandy' and 'modern' and 'modernist', following his argument can be like trying to see a line of pebbles under a bank of fog. He treats wildly dissimilar phenomena – Mods, dandies, dandy Mods and modernist dandies – as though they were the same thing. (Even at the time, many original modernists spurned Mod as a moody knock-off, a Carnaby Street caricature – wayward ideas replaced by winking insignia and a price tag on everything.)

Weight is so stuck on his through-line map that he never stays long enough to see the strangeness of the scenes he's passing through. (I'm tempted here by the neologism 'tellyology'. Definition: shaping history with both eyes on a potential TV series.) I suspect the book he really wanted to write was a social history of Britain as seen through its subcultures, but these days books need hooks, and that's where Mod comes in. Or rather, where Mod goes out, because rather than looking again at the rich and paradoxical details of each Mod-ish stage, Weight is always pushing on to the next 'Mod-influenced' or 'Mod favourite' thing, from 'Golden Egg restaurants' to the 'Mod-inflected British rock group Kaiser Chiefs'. The links can be tenuous, to say the least. Jean-Luc Godard gets in for *A Bout de souffle*. OK, but Weight makes it sound like *Summer Holiday* with Gitanes and avant-garde haircuts. Alain Delon gets two mentions – one for a Smiths sleeve, the other for being an early scooter adopter. (None for his revenant gangster in Melville's *Le Samouraï*, which may be the most Mod film ever made: narcissism as narcotic, style as armour, and a fatal crush on a young black nightclub singer.) The 'beautifully dressed' Marcello Mastroianni makes the cut, because he 'embodied the modern, urban European male in films like Fellini's *La Dolce Vita* and Antonioni's *La Notte*'. You'd think these films were a freewheeling wolf-whistle breeze, when in fact their 'modern, urban European male' is flesh-spoiled, jagged with anomie, lagging behind his own heartbeat. He may be sharply dressed but he's losing traction. Weight's tick 'em off method makes everything sound like fashion PR: he catches the surface glimmer but misses any warning flares about imminent decadence. He honours some art-house films because they were one of the ways Mods 'absorbed ... the Continental lifestyle'. I'd like to have heard more from ex-Mods, in their own words, about the honeymoon experience of seeing such odd, uneasy

30

films. (Weight takes one quote from Terry Rawlings's book *Mod: A Very British Phenomenon*. Hmmm, catchy title, what?) By stressing fashion over ideas, Weight sacrifices an important thread: he makes young working-class Mods sound like boys who will cross an entire continent for the right pair of socks, but don't have an idea in their heads.

The Beatles' crucial role in the American Invasion of the mid-1960s becomes 'the mediation of Mod-related music and fashion to young Americans'. The Kinks are duly ticked off as a Mod band (in Weightese, 'figureheads who in their music, dress and interviews articulated Mods' outlook') when they were never really Mods, or hippies or anything very easy to pin down. What they were was awfully odd from the get-go, their echoic lack of definition precisely why they were so singular at the time and still sound so convulsively fresh today. If Ray Davies was a Mod, it was only one of many pre-emptive masks he sported. (And 'sported' is definitely the word.) The Union Jack draped around the Kinks was thorny collage not breezy appliqué. Beneath the lilt and fizz of the group's sound, Davies's fashion slaves and ladies' men are a dodgy lot, North London stand-ins for Mastroianni's self-hypnotized Casanova. In 'Dandy' the larky bedhopper is sent up, then stripped to pieces. But what's really nagging at Davies here is the passage of time: 'You lowdown dandy, you can't escape the past / Are you feeling old now?' Davies already had a ticcy eye on the clock. Success had no sooner spread its gold lamé legs for him than he was pouting: 'Where have all the good times gone?' He sounds tired of waiting but truly petrified of the uncertain fate at waiting's end.

I spent a recent coastal holiday listening to the Kinks'

back catalogue and was mesmerized all over again. (I wanted to do the same with the Who, but all I found in the motorway services' rack was an audiobook of Pete Townshend reading his recent autobiography: a whole 15 CDs' worth. I'm sorry – no one, not even a freelancer, has that much leisure time.) A half-century on, it's difficult to recapture the tingly shock of Davies's quicksilver voice in its original context, but that still doesn't explain or excuse how the Kinks, like Mod, are being turned into a paisley signifier for reassuring nostalgia. There's a whole other story here but Weight can't, or won't, hear it. For one thing, he needs to hurry along to match the Kinks up with mid-1990s Britpop. We don't ever learn if the similarity goes very deep, but it's one of those now obligatory pop-heritage coach stops. It has to be said (except Weight doesn't say it) that Blur's 'Country House' already sounds more dated than anything from a sunny afternoon in 1966. But here they all are, stirred into the same pot: the Who, the Kinks, Blur, Oasis. Here's 'Noel Gallagher playing his trademark guitar', the word 'trademark' an unhappy, if telling, choice. Here's a photo of Blur where they 'display their Mod influences in Clacton in 1993'. Though some of the 1960s groups doubtless spent happy time in Clacton as kids, it's unlikely that Blur had ever set foot there before this stagey photo op with an 'iconic' white Jag. As for any display of Mod influences, I'm baffled. They look like what they are, which is – no offence – scruffy students slumming it. There is nothing on show that screams, or whispers, Mod. Listen – they're speaking gap year Esperanto: Dr Martens boots, charity shop jackets, indie badges, NHS glasses and studiously just-fell-out-of-bed hair. Damon Albarn tries to do a bit of a Pinkie Brown psych-ward glare but it's pitiable – a strong breeze would knock him over. And is that shirt unironed? Mod! You mugging me off? It's four art-school herberts leaning against a car that's not their own in a world that's not their own, that refers to precisely nothing outside itself except other half-digested references. Just out of frame is a tacky Essex nightclub called Oscar's, complete with a big fake blow-up Academy Award statuette. This does seem apt.

Noel Gallagher has a tiny bit more claim to Mod bona fides, although Oasis's boilerplate music – where the Flintstone rock aesthetic rules supreme, to a point just short of prophylaxis – seems about as far from the original cosmopolitan dream of Mod as it's possible to get. Weight is untroubled by these lacunae: if it looks like Mod and walks like Mod it goes on the lightbox. (A quick aside on the photos: if nothing else, you would expect this to be a major treat in a book about Mod, but there are notably few images of real Mods among the cross-section of rock groups, fashion shoots, book covers, a snap of Bowie from his least Mod phase and a recent Bradley Wiggins mag cover. Actual Mods in the wild? Nothing. A tabloid snap of Mods scattering Rockers on Margate beach is a distant seagull's eye view of blurry matchstick men. An after-hours photo that purports to show a Mod couple in a 1960s club also frames a stray can of Hofmeister, which suggests the pic was taken much later.)

Mod's 'very British style' was initially a tasteful synthesis of American flash and European savoir faire. By the time of the first Mod revival in 1979, the once omnivorous sensibility felt moody and shopsoiled – a Mod Airfix kit, complete with decals. All the arrows turned sharply inward. Mrs T had logged 14 months in Downing Street by the time revival-barkers the Chords released what amounted to a manifesto-lite, a 45 called

'The British Way of Life', which does sound rather like a kids-are-alright re-voicing of Thatcher's 'Where there is doubt, may we bring faith'. It is this Little Englander, stodge-with-everything revivalism that means Mod is now often seen as hopelessly backward-looking, beached, a sad hobbyhorse. I'm not sure how aware Weight is of this – he certainly underplays the extent to which 'zombie' Mods are mocked and reviled in the pop media. 'Mod revival' is used as shorthand for a ploddy, meat-and-potatoes rock conservatism: so-called 'dad rock', with Paul Weller its peacock-suited John Major. (Even in the mid-1960s, Mod was already partial to raspy, gimme-gimme singers like Steve Marriott, and what was considered their more 'authentic' grain of voice.)

Today, we're again in the middle of a full-blown Mod revival. If you take the trouble to follow a few Mod-related Twitter feeds, you'll discover a scene in boisterously rude health. (First impression: it's far more laddish, not at all ambisexual and far less of an aesthete's playground than the original scene.) Every weekend there's a clutch of events to choose from – coastal get-togethers galore. This marks, what, a fourth or fifth generation re-revival? There are tribute bands who have tribute bands. There are original bands with no original members in their line-up. Getting a set from pantomime ska band Bad Manners is considered a real coup de théâtre. What this looks like, from the outside, is a postmodern end-of-the-pier show. Beer and scooters. And yet, while it's easy to sneer at its degraded state, I'm torn. Part of me knows I'd have a pretty good time at some of these gatherings. By my third pale ale I'd be talking Big Youth and brogues with the best of 'em. I grew up with this stuff, it's in my blood: I hitch-hiked, full of Pro Plus, to the original Wigan Casino; I went to ridiculous lengths to get hold of import reggae and soul 45s. There are photos of me from 1979 in full Rude Boy fig. (I still miss that particular pork pie hat.) Scarily, bizarrely, I'm something like an elder of the tribe now.

But where Mod once gave off a jumpy static of something arcane, unstable, unreadable, it now betrays an air of fussy self-satisfaction: neat alphabetical rows of old 45s on the Immediate label; original pre-loved bowling shoes in polythene; repro vintage guitars and rebranded clothes lines. Sex and drugs and rock and soul, minus the crucial Dionysian spark. Mod has become something to collect, a subcult first edition. On a recent afternoon spent in the stagnant pool of daytime TV, I came across the renowned impressionist Rory Bremner (known for his 'sharp satire and unforgiving political commentary') giving himself over to a satirical – sorry, sartorial – makeover, in a Brighton boutique which specializes in everything Mod. The odd thing about this (OK, one of the odd things about this) was that, post-makeover, it was hard to see any real difference. Bremner must have started his day in the soft hands of a TV production company stylist anyway, plus he wears what everyone un-young and half-savvy wears these days – a nice mix of Paul Smith and Margaret Howell, I'd guess. There's no such thing as 'subculture' now, and there's definitely no real generation gap. Where Townshend and Davies once sang about the alien tea cosy world of mums and dads, by 1990 Shaun Ryder of the Happy Mondays could ruefully start a song: 'Son, I'm thirty.'

At this year's Glastonbury festival, young students danced to the seventy-year-old pied piper Mick Jagger, while their parents 'had it large' with shouty grime acts. For sure, there were odd pockets of tribal homo-geneity, but you'd have been hard-pushed to identify any of them as 'Mod-inflected'. You could argue we've never been less 'Mod-inflected'. We're all about the casual tracksuit and the ripped denim shorts, rather than suits and ties; we're shamelessly confessional rather than broodingly cool; we're ad hoc tattooed rather than buttoned-up tight. 'We are all modernists now,' Weight says. (I don't think he means we're all Charlie Parker fans, though it's a nice thought.) One problem with this is that he's celebrating the continuity of something that no longer exists. As a result of Mod, he says, 'it is true to say that more British people came to see themselves as modern than ever before'. Sure, fine, maybe, even if that 'ever before' feels a bit fudgy. As a result of Mod (and the newly hot postwar electric media), a group like the Who could reach millions of people in one lightning-flash TV appearance. A kind of modernity was also what cool 1950s jazz and jittery 1960s rock had in common: they dared their audiences to measure themselves and their world against the music's stark or playful, soft or apocalyptic new tones. But what exactly was being illuminated here? What were the strange codes passing back and forth between audience and stage? And why was there such disappointment and introspection and withdrawal later on? Doesn't the more basic point concern not so much this or that movement or scene, as the very idea of 'seeing ourselves'? Wasn't this the real modernist key change?

At the end of a numb day spent with Weight's snap-happy Lego of statistics, I put on Miles Davis's *Kind of Blue* in an attempt to really hear it again, to catch the original lure through all the intervening time-fuzz. I say 'original', but by the time I came to it *Kind of Blue* was already 15 years old – it's harder still to imagine how it signified in 1959. How can something so feathery and frosty and rapt still cause such deep shock? It may be hard to believe, now that it's become an everywhere gastropub soundtrack, but hearing music like this for the first time could be a dizzying, even upsetting experience. Yes, it contains a sense of hard-won joy – but also sharp overtones of siege and fear, loss and regret. If *Kind of Blue* was a specifically modern achievement, it's in part because the players were unafraid of the deafening silence at the edge of their sound. There were darker, more jagged emotions under the elegant façade, something beyond hot trends and cool shades. I instinctively distrust any over-reliance on the word 'soul' in music criticism, but it's the only word that comes to mind here, a code word for all sorts of dreams and difficulties. For anyone back then, 1959 or 1974, raised in a UK household where neither introspection nor exuberance were madly encouraged, where home life was a cramped, stifling affair, and where you didn't have a ready-made language for certain unruly feelings, music like this could really melt the inherited chip of ice in the heart. It still can.

Interviewed after he'd left the *Kind of Blue* line-up, the pianist Bill Evans said: 'The simple things, the essences, are the great things, but our way of expressing them can be incredibly complex.' Evans was a neurasthenic-looking white boy in an all-black band, a man with a bruised, lyrical sensibility in a world that could be blithe, even brutish. You could spend years exploring Evans's sublime solo work, trying to work out why his playing – which can seem gossamer-light, one register away from rosy banality – is so haunting. Evans looked at times like an algebra professor who'd walked onto the wrong stage. He had the classy Ivy League suit and never a hair out of place, but his private life was a hurtling fugue, a circular to-and-fro of self-cancelling feints and narcotic stratagems. The arrows here all point inward, after the manner of St Sebastian. 'The simple things you see...'

It may be unrealistic to expect a zippy book like Weight's to delve into such areas, but the complete absence of any depth or surprise feels wearyingly familiar from recent TV. There, bland retrospectives suck on past lives and leach all the contrary gristle and blood from their hard-won victories. 'From the boutiques of Brighton to the aisles of Ikea... modernism strutted its stuff.' Weight's spayed, odourless jargonese is to real analysis what a TV makeover or a 'scooters only' weekender in Margate in 2013 are to the original modernist dare: a perfectly glossy simulation, with all risky elements stowed.

Just as empty shipyards now house 'themed' museums – press icon for 'Virtual Wage Packet Experience' – so the insane over-ambition of mid-1960s pop and rock has been repackaged as a tidily groovy heritage resource. In the British Music Experience, for example, installed (where else?) in the former Millennium Dome and created 'to fill a gap in the UK Heritage Sector for rock and pop music', what did they choose as a logo? Right first time: the 'classic', 'iconic' RAF/Mod target emblem. Among the artefacts on show is Noel Gallagher's 'trademark' Union Jack guitar. To be sure, rock groups themselves are often complicit in this process – it's probably hard not to be these days.[1] 'Perhaps, in that sense,

1   Recently seen on Twitter: 'NOW AVAILABLE: The Who Fortieth Anniversary Quadrophenia Co-Lab Tour Parka'. Further details at the online Who shop: 'Fishtail parka based on the iconic M-1951 US Army Parka. £299.99'.

we are all modernists now,' Weight (sort of) concludes. Really? How do the intense ardour and idealism of all those modernist dreams live on in the freeze-dried clamour of postmodernism? Are we really all modernists now? Sometimes we look more like the bloodless archivists of a real gone time.

DID HE FEEL GOOD?
JAMES BROWN'S EPIC LIFE AND CAREER

James Brown's legendary reputation as the Hardest Working Man in Show Business was part virile boast and part canny PR. Had a bad week at work? The Man will give you a show to raise your spirits and cancel out the pain. He put as much work into his act as his audience put into their low-end jobs. Showbiz was man's work, hard labour, as much sweat of his brow as swish of his cape. The audience got its money's worth; and if Brown understood one thing above all else, it was the many uses and values, financial and symbolic, of money. He never went on tour without a big bag of ready cash – to grease wheels, ameliorate tensions, make obstacles disappear. After he died, people found boxes of dollar bills stashed in the walls of his house, or buried out back on his land.

Born in 1933, Brown learned his hard-headed ways in a 1950s music business that was a rough twine of Mafia hegemony and outta-sight profits. He believed in the redemptive power of hard work as others believed in the blood of the lamb. A true believer in the do-it-yourself ethos of the American Dream, he didn't see why race should be a barrier to getting the good things in life. Hard work was how he shaped his destiny in a sectarian world, his eventual success the product of near tyrannical drive and will. He could be hard work personally, too. He rarely took no for an answer, whether it was a question of getting an encore, sleeping with him, or signing away your royalties. In his music as in his wiles, Brown was no suave pinkie-ring seducer. He had none of the snake-charmer sweetness of a later generation of soul men. If the key to musical seduction is hiding all artifice behind a carefully dishevelled front of natural élan, Brown took another road, emphasizing all the stuff other artists tucked away. Listening to Brown's classic hits – 'Cold Sweat', 'Out of Sight', 'Get Up (I Feel Like Being A) Sex Machine' – you could be eavesdropping on some 11th-hour rehearsal, the air jumpy with back-chat, barked instructions, and flip, musicianly code. You can all but hear the effort that goes into summoning up the bumpy and volatile groove.

Brown's music seems fully dependent on its front man, entirely led by his sandpaper rasp – but if you want to dig its secret flow, you have to listen down past Brown himself into a song's boiler-room frequencies, where the bass and drums make things shake. If you've always been baffled by just what it is a bass player does, play 'Sex Machine' and try tuning your ear to the sin-uously pivotal bass line William 'Bootsy' Collins lays down; bass and guitar supply the song's true harmony, with Brown's vocalizing so much scattershot percus-sion. This music is hard work, in the best sense: you can feel the sweat, see the crooked smiles on the musicians' faces. It seems to bypass all rationale and go straight to the sacroiliac, its emphasis never quite where you expect it to be. Brown had his own code for this hypnotic way of playing off the beat: he called it The One.

Which is ostensibly what the title of this new biog-raphy of Brown, *The One*, by music writer R. J. Smith, alludes to – though it carries a supplementary meaning of the one and only, the exception to all normal rules. And at his peak, Brown was a country mile of contra-dictions. He preached black revolution but courted Republican power brokers. He loved being honoured as Black Businessman of the Year, but his investments failed and he stubbornly resisted paying taxes. He needed to be loved and feted in his hometown Georgia neighbourhood even as sullen murmurs persisted in the community about unpaid bills and broken promises. He craved public respectability but privately behaved like a Mafia chieftain. He wanted to be seen as a strong and dependable father figure but appears to have had no truck with the wearisome daily reality of raising kids. Officially, Brown had nine children with three or four different women (and some disputed additional off-spring). For political reasons as much as anything else, Brown wanted to be perceived as the opposite of a part-time, deadbeat dad, but he seems to have been baffled by children – their presence, their spontaneity, their need for casual affection.

Brown himself had a horrific childhood even by the standards of the time – no real childhood at all, in fact. He went straight from the cradle to the street, where he got a street-corner education in amoral, get-it-any-way-you-can wheel and deal. Like Richard Pryor and Billie Holiday, he learned the relative valuations of love and money in a relative's whorehouse. Perhaps because he didn't have a childhood proper – a place of safety, play, and the unhurried formation of certain shared recog-nitions – this space remained empty and replete with anxiety for him. He couldn't play with his own chil-dren, because he had never learned to play himself. For Brown, play was always work, but work was never play. You get a consonant feeling from the music: even at its most avowedly merciful or pleading, his songs carry an almost dementedly wilful, near-threatening charge.

This bad start in life shaped his relationships with adults as well. Brown mostly preferred the company of people who inhabited the shady middle ground between hard work and outright hustle. He liked to test his wits against characters he knew were trying to outmanoeuvre him. He liked reptilian crooks and scurvy knaves, especially if they were white and Southern. (One of his most enduring – in fact only enduring – friendships was with, of all people, the wily and indestructible Southern politician Strom Thurmond.) He had a fatal weakness for beady-eyed chancers who didn't have his best interests at heart, but he treated family and band members with feudal scorn and feigned incomprehension. In the long run this proved fatal, both personally and financially.

One close associate quoted by Smith says Brown was 'exceptionally slick and conniving and he made sure – made sure – he was misunderstood'. With Brown, you couldn't win. If you went along with his mind games, you were a weakling. If you stood up to him, you were exiled. When people eventually realized they were damned in either case, many walked away. (Some of the stories here can break the heart – including the daughter frozen out because she broke ranks and tried to get her father help for his various problems late in life.) Brown wouldn't be told how to act. 'You can't tell me / how to run my mess!' he sang, or insisted, like a mantra. In the early days, this meant spurning the advice of white agents and managers to tone down the sheer blackness of his act. Later on, it meant not mouthing the safe ideological line reigning black power-brokers had prepared for him. Brown did make sure he was crystal clear on certain issues. 'I Don't Want Nobody to Give Me Nothing (Open Up The Door I'll Get It Myself)' is less a song title than an embryonic policy paper. He dubbed himself the Funky President, and in most important respects, he was a stand-alone black conservative: anti-drug, pro-school, anti-revolution, pro–hard work.

He urged black people not to riot. He was deeply

suspicious of using the apologia of societal racism to excuse inertia or failure. In Brown's world, you only had yourself to blame or praise. A man was what a man did: he had to step out there into a hostile world and shape it according to his own desires. Brown had no truck with blaming whitey; he was at war with destiny itself. In this sense, he was colour-blind. Nothing and no one would halt the procession of his irresistible will. A part of this was mere grandstanding (one more street-theatre way of getting the crowd to stop and look at him), but it also went deeper, provoking serious disaffection within his core black audience.

In 1972, Brown supported Richard Nixon for re-election over his challenger George McGovern because he liked the president's policy of New Federalism. Nixon depicted the Democratic faith in big government as only skin-deep in its equity, being in reality deeply patronizing to anyone a few rungs down the socioeconomic ladder. Nixon presented his initiative as a way of putting start-up money where it should be: in the hands of states and individuals, not Washington. This harmonized with Brown's own street-level ethic: he didn't think black people should get any special breaks. Every black man could be a Brown man and make his dreams palpable if he put his mind to it. For Brown, there was more nobility in screwing money out of fools than in being given it for free. (He was distrustful of welfare and affirmative action because they catered to blacks en masse, where he considered himself special, incomparable, chosen: the One.) For Brown, there was no paradox in talking about Black Pride but privately demanding an appearance fee for same. If you came from poor, you went where the dollars were. And Brown put his money where his mouth was, opening up several businesses in black neighbourhoods. He bought and overhauled radio stations, promoted other artists, started fast-food chains tailored to black appetite and aesthetics. Everything was done with daemonic flair (including the bookkeeping, unfortunately).

Brown stuck by Nixon, even when black Democrats organized a Brown boycott, black media mocked his supposed Uncle Tom-ism, and his audience did a slow fade. Later came another 45 with a pimped-out paren-thesis: 'You Can Have Watergate (Just Gimme Some Bucks and I'll Be Straight)'. This was always Brown's bottom line: have you got the bucks or don't you? Money was both the motor and the proof of self-im-provement. Money, not social upheaval, was the key to freedom. His proudest boast was being a 'perfect symbol of black entrepreneurship', encouraging a whole nation of black-owned businesses like his own. 'Now brother – DON'T – leave your homework undone,' sang Brown on 'I'm a Greedy Man'. But businesses can't stay afloat on symbolic pizzazz alone, and one after another, his investments crashed. Brown loved the idea of being chairman of the board, but he had neither the time nor the small-print aptitude for what that job involved. (It probably didn't help that his formative years on the road gave him a combative idea of business ethics not taught at Harvard: a Colt .45 in his belt and deep pockets for filing returns.)

Consider again that quote above. Brown calls himself a symbol of black entrepreneurship. And as a symbol alone he was golden, preaching a gospel of being real, standing tall, even if no one can run an empire on such feel-good generalities (though talkin' loud and say-in' nothing is not bad training for running a modern political campaign). Brown also had to carry the same burden as other successful blacks, who found it was not enough to be brilliant in their chosen field. They also had to be 24/7 community role models. This could surely drive anyone crazy – without the added complication of different sections of the community wanting entirely incompatible role models. Succeed one way and people will call you a sell-out. Stick to your base and others will say you haven't been adventurous enough. Get your affairs in order and you'll be called an Oreo. Don't take care of financial business and people will sigh: same old lazy-ass story.

In the 1970s, just as his business ventures were failing, things started faltering for Brown artistically, too. The soul music he'd helped fashion was enjoying a huge artistic renaissance. Popularity hit an all-time high in sales, artistic daring, and crossover success, as black artists – Marvin Gaye, Stevie Wonder, the O'Jays, among many others – exploited and overhauled the LP format, producing gorgeous, resonant, suite-like worlds of sound. Brown came from a time when the concert tour, more than the studio, was the real work, and maybe he needed that instant audience feedback. All the great hits of Brown's 60s and 70s heyday were seven-inch singles at a time when 45s were made and consumed like so many sonic headlines. Taken together, those 45s were like an alternative news wire or TV station. A volley of wild and wanton ricochets, they provided unforgettable catch phrases ('Say it Loud! I'm Black and I'm Proud!' 'Get on the Good Foot!'), along with unlikely black superheroes like Mister Super Bad and the New Minister of the Super Heavy Funk. Brown couldn't (or wouldn't) make the switch to the LP-centred aesthetic. He did one thing and he did it well, and after a certain point he stopped responding effectively to change. It was one thing to grow out his Afro and cheerlead for Black Pride – some vital chamber in his thorny heart could beat loudly behind that mission. When he tried to hustle up a patchy enthusiasm for passing trends like disco and rap, the results were brittle, self-parodic, and unconvincing.

Brown made new shapes for American music, but they were shapes that moved the body and massaged the id. How much they touched the heart is another matter. Brown's best music is an electrifying flare of movement, power, and hunger, but it's not music you play at home to lose yourself in. When Smith says the music of Brown's contemporaries 'sounds finished, whereas Brown's still mystifies', it seems to me that he has things exactly the wrong way round. Brown's music does a lot of things, but it never mystifies. (It never reaches into the mystic, either.) It is profoundly anti-mystification: with a bit of practice, any listener can hear the rig under its highway grind. There's a lot of showbiz cheek and feint going on, too, which isn't necessarily a criticism. You can't expect any man to scream and plead and cry, authentically, night by night, tour by tour, year on year, for a lifetime – even if that's precisely what many Brown fans would love to believe.

Smith notes how a new audience – younger, hipper, whiter – started coming to Brown's 1980s shows, expecting to hear the band that made all those killer 45s. What they got was cummerbunds and tired showbiz routine. Smith offers a telling anecdote from Bootsy Collins – the brilliant young bassist who got his start with 'Sex Machine'-era Brown but soon tired of the rip-off and run-around and left the JB orbit, first into the mad empire of George Clinton and then on to solo success with his own outfit, Bootsy's Rubber Band. Brown bumped into Bootsy on the road, as the fortunes of the One were dipping, and the other rising. The only thing Brown had to say to his ex-protégé was: 'How can you call yourselves a *band*, boy? You don't even wear matching suits!' He wasn't joking.

Brown could fake a lot of things, but he couldn't fake vulnerability or regret or confusion. He didn't do weakness or softness. He was James Brown! He was the One, and he always got what he wanted. Unlike other troubled soul-men like Marvin Gaye and Al Green, Brown had no Church in his soul. Sure, he put over some songs like an old-time preacher, but that was projective shtick, just like he borrowed bits of flash from drag queens and tap dancers in the street. He didn't need God because he worshipped at his own rugged altar. His ego was impregnable. His music doesn't have the carnal/devotional tension that marks the work of the greatest soul singers, many of whom were made personally unhappy by its grip but found a way to project the spiritual malaise into songs of unearthly bliss and strangeness. What's missing from Brown's music is any hint or breath of otherness, sweetness, light. His is a roar of certainty, done deals, and finality.

Smith is thrillingly good on Brown's sound, on the meaning and place of all his different screams, licks, and riffs. There is some great writing here about how Brown worked (and played) the recording studio, how songs fell or fidgeted together in improvised studio jams. (If 'songs' is what they are: Brown at his most characteristic is less a singer than someone who exhorts, declaims, and extemporizes – sometimes brilliantly, sometimes at the very edge of buzz-word vacuity.) At the time, this was a revolutionary way of putting music together

48

(Miles Davis, among others, was listening closely), but Smith never quite dares the question of how much credit Brown deserves as against the claims of his various musicians. Brown's studio sessions had no musical 'charts': Brown would hum a riff or issue a gnomic utterance regarding the mood he wanted, and it was up to the band to make it happen. Out of all the things Brown signifies, it's his music that's had the strongest afterlife: the actual sound of the One, its churning, jumpy, iterative texture. If Brown stalks rap and hip-hop and other hideouts of contemporary sound, it's not through his vocal glory so much as what turntable mavens call the 'breaks': the never-bettered short-order alchemy of drums, bass, guitar, and horns. There's a parallel here with Bob Marley and 1970s reggae. While high-brow critics devote books to Marley as natural mystic and ideological poet – Che Guevara with a Gibson guitar – it's the edgy bricolage of dub and DJ talk-over that has claimed the cultural day, not the radical preacher man's get-together, love-one-another jive.

Smith notes that Brown's musicians never got their fair share of credit or royalties, but in the end he falls back on the safe idea that without Brown, none of it would have happened. While that's certainly true of the extraordinary live show Brown put together in the 1950s and early 1960s – which exploded into the homes of un-black America via Brown's white-hot TV appearance on The T.A.M.I. show of 1964 – the recorded music remains a grey area. Brown could be an inspired conductor of chaos, but he could also be slapdash, meagre, and funky-by-rote. In the doldrums of the 70s, he had a great opportunity to get back in the musical spotlight when producers wanted him to provide the soundtrack for a key 'Blaxploitation' movie. He scrabbled together some outtakes from his studio archive and didn't even bother to re-program them before posting them off. Brown's then-bandleader, Fred Wesley, felt sorry for his boss – who was obviously too tired and troubled and busy to do his best – so Wesley personally wrote, played, and produced a whole new instrumental score for the film from scratch. The producers loved it. Brown was outraged and fired Wesley on the spot.

It's a miracle how Smith manages to keep the telling of this increasingly sad, grubby, violent tale so buoyant. It's a book I didn't want to stop reading, even as part of me wanted what I was reading about to stop happening. Smith never pontificates. His story grabs you and won't let go, just like the best of Brown's music. It's only afterward that you may feel a bit cheated that Smith kept quiet about all the wider resonances of Brown's behaviour. If you never suspect that this is a white guy hedging his moral bets because he's writing the life of a huge black icon, you do sense that Smith got more of an education than he wanted in undoing the buttons and stays of this taxing modern life. If Smith is disappointed in Brown the man, he keeps it to himself: he simply lays out the evidence, leaving it to us to draw our own conclusions.

Mostly, those conclusions don't reflect well on Brown or anyone who tended the myth down the years. Brown ripped off his bands – not through inattention but deliberately, peevishly; he beat up girlfriends and wives – not occasionally, but repetitively, recreationally, sometimes viciously; he neglected and then froze out his children; he... well, at this point you put the book down and go play the music again to remind yourself why you're bothering. If you haven't been put off the music for good, that is.

Maybe all subsequent problems were the result of a simple category error: when someone who was a brilliant showbiz act was proclaimed an important socio-political spokesman. It wasn't so much in his songs as his very being that Brown's importance as a figurehead lay. Brown was black, and loud, and proud, and successful, and in-your-face unrepentant at a time when just being quietly and submissively black could get you overnight jail time. This is the one area where Brown's arrogance worked for the good: he demanded his part of the American Pie. But how does what is permissible on stage – wild abandon, exaggerated claims, world-encircling desire – find a roost in the grey maze of real life? Being proclaimed a prophet as much as a showbiz phenomenon may involve more hubris than any one man can handle.

And then, at the age of 52, Brown – who had been virtually drug-abstinent his whole life – took a bewildering swan-dive into the depths of drugged-out madness: he contracted a heavy and coarsening addiction to PCP (a.k.a. Angel Dust), a drug avoided by all but the most desperate street addicts. Even pre-PCP, Brown seems always to have been in motion, a multi-tasking blur for whom downtime was just a different form of work. This sudden and escalating intake of PCP meant his legendary testiness began to shade into genuine paranoia. He thought the trees on his estate had been co-opted by the FBI to capture his speech. A long-established gun fetish effloresced into trigger-happy mania. All sorts of stuff which had been kept under control (and under wraps) for decades suddenly exploded into public disgrace.

After one day of drug-stoked, gun-waving madness, Brown found himself facing real jail time. He had threatened members of the public he thought had used his office restroom without permission and then took the local police on a long car chase across state lines. When they finally ran his speeding vehicle to ground, Brown stepped from his pick-up truck, spread his gargantuan hands, and started singing 'Georgia on My Mind'. It was only now that Brown lapsed into the sort of racial conspiracy-speak he would once have execrated. (There was a time he would rather have said nothing than solicit pity.) A huge outcry went up when he was finally jailed – how could the United States incarcerate someone like James Brown! What other country on earth? Had nothing changed? The truth was less dramatic and more squalid. Brown could consider himself lucky to have stayed out of jail for as long as he did. In the previous year alone, he'd been arrested seven times. Not only were there second-nature patterns of spousal (and other) abuse, ready violence, and tax avoidance, but there was, equally, a lifelong pattern of cover-up. Bad things had been buried, excused, and euphemized for half a lifetime.

Brown didn't need to go to jail: all he had to do was plead guilty and he would have got off with a fine and lip-service rehab. But according to his own dilatory logic, it was better to be perceived a jail-bound martyr than to let his fans know he was a powerless addict. And once incarcerated, it was better (both for sales and his image) to play the inglorious race card and imply some racist setup, though plenty of whites (including his faithful friend, Thurmond) had done their best to ensure Brown's liberty. It was his own choice to go to jail, to exploit the sorry situation with wink-wink insinuations that, hell, no white superstar would have faced such indignities. On another occasion, he pulled a literally unbelievable 'I'm just a poor dumb coloured boy' act to get around paying his back taxes. (Again, no conspiracy was involved; he undoubtedly owed what the IRS said he owed, probably more.) In a bizarre letter to the White House, Brown floated a risible line of sophistry: 'You can only be a tax evader if you have intent. But seeing as I'm just this poor unschooled black man, I couldn't possibly have such clever intent.' The letter is so wily it obviates its own premise.

Did a tired and disappointed Brown take PCP to feel how the younger Brown felt when normal? A fellow abuser's comment that the drug is like 'giving yourself a nervous breakdown' seems telling. Maybe after 30 years of being the driving force, the new black paradigm, the funky rule to which there was no exception, this elective chemical detour was one way Brown saw of dissipating the joyless pressure of always being the One. Maybe he needed a nervous breakdown – a long-postponed holiday from rigour, machismo, having always to be 'on'. It has a kind of logic: you get to go crazy while insisting it's only the chemical genie making you that way. Just because he was the epitome of funky doesn't mean that the underlying ethos in Brownsville wasn't unrelentingly rational, martial, and unyielding. From the beginning, everything was strictly choreographed and repeated every night to the same inch-perfect degree. (It was not enough that band members had their shoes shined; it had to be the right kind of shine, or they got docked pay.) Smith is acute on how even the wildest peaks of a Brown performance were actually closely practised and drilled. Under the starry cape, he carried around his own suit of heavy, impenetrable armour.

Brown's story surely illustrates the dark side of the American Dream – paranoid, reclusive, self-cancelling – that can be seen in wildly divergent figures across the ideological spectrum, from Howard Hughes and Hunter S. Thompson to Elvis Presley and Michael Jackson. (Is it mere coincidence that Brown and Thompson were both attracted, in their different ways, to the same paranoiac nemesis and compadre – Richard Milhous Nixon?) Having it all doesn't make the winner happy; if anything, it turns you into a permanent sentry at the CCTV gateway to your own life, waiting for raiding parties and enemies and ragged ghosts. Brown died a lonely old man, self-sufficiency become a Midas curse. He never stopped touring, right to the end – though it's unclear if he did so because he enjoyed it, or because without it there was nothing else, or because on the financial front, he'd finally outwitted even himself and couldn't afford to stop. Was any of it fun? Did he know what fun or contentment was? Brown had trained himself to keep singing, keep smiling, keep screaming I FEEL GOOD, when he perhaps felt nothing of the sort. Who do you run to, who do you tell, when you realize you've built a prison out of the things you thought were liberations?

Brown died in the same small patch of South Carolina where he was born. In his front room, in later years, he kept African slave shackles and sprigs of cotton for ornament. You wonder if the incredible journey he mapped finally took him very far out of his original bedrock orbit. 'For me, the American Dream has been fulfilled,' he remarks, in one of his various autobiographies. He got everything he ever wanted, but life only seemed to get harder and meaner and more melancholy. In that sense, the life has a familiar classical shape: the Hardest Working Man in Show Business rubbed up against the worst dreams of men and ultimately paid a heavy, soul-consuming price. This fable of the One contains many cautions, and here is just one: following the council of your high-riding id may make for a wild and electric rise, but expect a deeply lonely and haunted final act.

POSTSCRIPT. I haven't changed a word of this 2012 review, but I should note that since then I've read at least three other views of Brown's life, and – especially – his final years, which have different takes on such vexed questions as why he ended up in jail; how he became addicted to PCP and who might have been supplying said drugs; and who might have stood to profit from his demise. You could start with the chapter on Brown in Stanley Booth's excellent *Rythm Oil*; move on to James McBride's 2016 *Kill 'Em and Leave: Searching For The Real James Brown*; and then try Googling an exhaustive 2019 CNN report that alleges, among other things, that Brown may have been murdered and that his ex-wife Adrienne may not have died of an accidental overdose. At the moment his legacy stands, uneasily tensed, between those institutions wanting to proclaim Brown as an inspirational black icon; and disturbing allegations of rape, assault, and drug abuse.

BIRDITIS: THE OBSESSION WITH CHARLIE PARKER

There was a lot of racial tension around bebop. Black men were going with fine, rich white bitches. They were all over these niggers out in public and the niggers were clean as a motherfucker and talking all kind of hip shit.

Trane liked to ask all these motherfucking questions back then about what he should or shouldn't play. Man, fuck that shit –

Bird had this white bitch in the back of the taxi with us. He'd done already shot up a lot of heroin and now –

There is a long and slightly disreputable tradition in jazz of oral biography. The 'as told to' voice here belongs to Miles Davis, in *Miles: The Autobiography*, first published in 1989 and officially attributed to 'Miles Davis with Quincy Troupe' (see also *Lady Sings the Blues* by 'Billie Holiday with William Duffy'). Depending on mood, ethnicity, ideology, drug of choice, an oral biography can strike the reader as an authentic reproduction of voice, in all its self-contradictory rhythm and curl – or borderline racist, like some Victorian anthropologist's respectably freaky show and tell.

A couple of things should be made clear: one, Quincy Troupe is a black poet and academic, not some ofay hack-cum-hustler; two, *Miles: The Autobiography* was released at a time when Davis was looking to get a little payback on his place in the tradition. He had those storm-warning eyes of his on the emerging rap/R&B/CD-reissue marketplace, and his bad-mouth persona didn't hurt the book's profile. Davis grew up in a stable middle-class home: his father was a hard-working dentist, a cultured and well-read man active in local politics; Miles attended Juilliard with a generous weekly allowance from Pops (enough, indeed, to help support an indigent Charlie Parker), and later hung out with writers and artists in post-war Paris. Consequently, some readers of *Miles: The Autobiography* found the mooted authenticity of a voice that felt like a brass-neck steal from Donald Goines's *Dopefiend* or Iceberg Slim's *Trick Baby* to be, at best, a balefully corny performance. On a deeper level, though, that voice hints at all sorts of unresolved tensions and uncomfortable truths about jazz and its place in post-war American life. How America sees – and hears – itself. How it imagines (or expects, demands) certain people sound. What truths it assigns to particular groups, while denying access to others.

Such tensions were manifest in jazz from the off, and reached a thorny apotheosis with the mid-century advent of the style known as bebop. (Bebop reset the spine of popular standards, vaulting off into a far more rarefied harmonic atmosphere.) Jazz may have been born and raised in brothels, gin joints, chthonic nightclubs, rather than respectable performance spaces, but it was a music of devilish complexity, exacting technical fibre. Musicians in touring jazz bands and orchestras had to satisfy the clamour of their weekend audience for beats that could be danced into the floor; satisfy their own high creative standards; and also find a way to leap unscathed between dense volleys of beckoning myth and image. In Charlie Parker's 1940s heyday jazz was one of the few spaces where black performers might carve out a life of relative artistic freedom, mostly on their own terms. How do you convey all the snares and banquets, peaks and deadfalls, of a difficult but intermittently joyous life like Parker's? You get on stage and blow, and shape something so expressive, so technically ferocious, so emotionally acute, it obviates any need for oh-by-the-way footnotes. Accept it, or don't: as existential fact it remains inviolable, undeniable. Unearthly sonic signatures woven from everyday air; flurries of notes like Rimbaud's million golden birds set free: no one else could do this one thing he did, exactly the way he did it.

Charlie Parker was one of the first deepwater jazz players to seize the public imagination. It may have taken a fateful early death in 1955 to settle his portion of true infamy, but mythic status was then assured. A plump, sharp-taloned Icarus in after-hours mufti, he was already the subject of a votive cult among bebop obsessives. Soon after his blurry end, aged 34, a fond graffito rose and sprouted all over New York: Bird Lives! Parker's sad extinction released myriad after-lives: musical colossus, modernist exemplar, contested emblem of racial politics, finally even the recipient of the paste crown of a posthumous Hollywood biopic. Parker's flinty, recondite music slowly shades into the background; he becomes better known for a ruinous pile-it-high lifestyle, for being the only addict pre-Fassbinder to get fatter, not thinner, as his habit deepens; for plunging into late decrepitude only to die in the lap of luxury, in a high-society eyrie belonging to the Rothschild child and 'Jazz Baroness', Pannonica de Koenigswarter.[2]

2   None of the three books under review disputes the untidy but now generally accepted version of the events surrounding Parker's death. So Hannah Rothschild's 2012 memoir, *The Baroness: The Search for Nica, the Rebellious Rothschild*, should berequired reading for anyone who always found that version more than a bit hinky. It turns out the attending doctor who

True believers want to reclaim Parker from a now (as they see it) deeply degraded image, emphasizing instead the dare and complexity of his music; this is already a gamble when many fairweather fans tend to shut down at the first mention of flattened fifths and roving thirteenths. Even if you've loved this music for half a lifetime, you can find the algebraic lingo of jazz theory about as clarifying as a book of logarithms baked in mud. Biographers first have to explain the tradition Parker emerged from – solo improvisation within a many-handed ensemble music – but also show Parker's own itchy, wasp-sting style as the fruit of one vulnerable life, no other. A life that was severely circumscribed, and correspondingly over intense. Stamen-soft pollen-dry old side-men, quoted in these biographies, testify that from early on the boy Parker was manifestly different: one of those characters who enter a room and social space instantly shapes itself around their fizzing tempo. Even contemporaries who never liked Parker don't try to deny it: he lit the workaday world on fire, left you wrung out and twitching. He took charge, ran rings, pulled the carpet out from under – both on and offstage. If you're going to flag the uncommon flair of Parker's playing via talk of chromatic scales and variant chords, you'd best find a way of doing so that doesn't

... notoriously supplied Parker's age as sixty-plus, not 34, was a high-society Dr Feelgood, dispensing magic narcotic shots to neurasthenic Park Avenue lady-addicts like Bird's pal the Jazz Baroness. Might Parker's death actually have been an OD, his already exhausted system unable to tolerate uncut medicinal heroin? This might account for a whole fistful of unexplained gaps in the various witness statements; also why a licensed physician might want Parker to appear older and frailer. There was perhaps more at stake for those left alive than the 'official' version has ever suggested.

wash the polydipsic chaos of the man out of the picture entirely. Parker's song was resolutely unsentimental, a sometimes harsh, hurtling thing: he put all his seducer's wiles into his life, not his music. So why does this spiky, astringent music touch so many of us, still?

In almost all the surviving photos of Parker, he sports what you would have to call a characteristic grin. Clean or stoned, upright or unsteady, in transit or out of reach, there it is again: a natural bodhisattva's airy acceptance of whatever's next. The full catastrophe! He seems to mingle contrary humours of unconcern and cupidity in one wobbly cartoon smile. There exists a snap from 1948 that shows Parker as pinstriped Michelin Man, behind who knows what speedball of bottles and tines, being euphemistically 'escorted' out of a club by prim drummer Max Roach and adoring disciple Dean Benedetti; a terminally dishevelled Bird, but the grin is intact, if anything even wider than usual – it looks alarmingly like victory.

William Burroughs said that you should never trust anyone who looked the same from photo to photo; Parker can appear a wholly different person across a single roll of film. In one snap he is spruce and trim, alight with boyish glee, like he just found a toy alto in his Xmas stocking; a few weeks later he's a slumped old man, bursting at the seams, a zoot-suit sofa set out on the kerb to disintegrate in the rain. Spend any time reviewing such images and you come to an unexpected conclusion: our supposed King of Cool is, if anything, notably un-'iconic'. In a bandstand snap from 1948 it's bassist Tommy Potter and a razor-cheeked young Miles who look like the hippest cadavers in town. In another band snap, from 1952, the likes of Oscar Peterson and

Ben Webster are prince-like, sunny, resplendent; Parker looks thirty years older than his 31 years, an ailing rhino in a crumpled suit. There is a shocking paparazzo pic from 1954 of Parker exiting a police van, entering Bellevue public hospital: filthy suit, shirt awry, trousers ridden up to his mottled knees. In *Celebrating Bird*, Gary Giddins includes three photos I'd never seen before, taken just before Parker's death. (Frustratingly, Giddins supplies no background context.) In one, Parker turns his back to the camera and covers his eyes, as if caught in a game of hide-and-seek. (Who with? Behind what shadows and posts?) In another, we see his reflection in a smeary nightclub mirror. In all, he appears spaced-out, placid, playful, gesturing from inside some deeply inaccessible personal beatitude. He looks like a happy ghost.

In my teens, I made my own portrait of Parker. It must have been circa 1975: a small town in Norfolk, a lacklustre grammar school, art A level. Parker's insanely cool milieu seemed a world as distant as the British Raj, or cowboys on the range. All my bebop reveries played in scratchy, staccato black and white. The Bird of my painting bursts into colour, if not life – he has the dubious solidity of a cheap garden-centre Buddha. The overworked surface is jagged to touch: piled-up arrowheads of paint, all blinding whites and golds, around the stony brown island of his face. I somehow caught something of the eyes: a flicker of American Indian ancestry, a musician's selfless self-absorption, a bit of junkie sag. But for all its mimed frenzy, the picture's a bit flat. The subject fills every last inch of pictorial space: no breathing space, nothing but Bird right to the edge of the frame. I was too young to work any kind of angle on the man's psychological fire or frailty. He feels way too close, yet still completely unreadable. Then again, there's part of me today thinks this isn't such a bad interpretation of the way things were with Bird.

At the time, I owned just the one Parker recording: *Charlie Parker on Dial: Volume 1*. The sleeve shot is a study in grey, Parker looming like an Easter Island god. The sleeve notes, by the Bird fanatic and Dial label founder Ross Russell (he later wrote the first Parker biography, published in 1973), detail a period on the West Coast in 1946 which produced agonies in Parker's life and a series of lustrous recordings. I still remember the several oily scenes Russell conjures up. Parker suffering acute heroin withdrawal in an airless LA garage: a metal cot, no heating, his thin spring coat the only scrap of warmth. He eats nothing for days on end, drowns himself in cheap booze. Later, he is found dazed and naked (bar socks and cigar) in a hotel lobby at midnight, and led back to his room three times. The long night finally ends when he nods off, the cigar sets his cheap mattress on fire, and the hotel has to be evacuated. In 1975, I read and reread this litany of stains and wounds and had my head turned around by the music and somehow it all seemed of a piece. None of it struck me as especially odd or extravagant or depressing.

Parker fell into the world in late summer 1920, on one side of the confluence of two muddy rivers. He was born in Kansas City (Kansas), before the family crossed the bridge to Kansas City (Missouri), which turned out to be provident ground for a future jazz-man. At the time, Kansas City was – in the parlance – 'wide open': there was an unofficial alliance between a corrupt police force and the wily, indefatigable crime boss Tom Pendergast. Giddins: 'Entertainment also flourished. The clubs and dance halls operated day and night, and the best musicians in the country were attracted as much by the competitive atmosphere ... as by the possibilities of employment.' There was no such thing as 'after hours': no time, day or night, when beady young comers couldn't find somewhere to hang out, catch musical giants at play, exchange lore, pick up soul-ageing work.

Parker was named for his father, Charles Parker Senior, a singer/dancer in the tough world of black vaudeville until an over-fondness for strong liquor precipitated a slow staggered decline. This seems to have been a man who drifted into (and out of) things: towns, marriages, jobs. He ended up working as a chef on a Pullman train. As with accounts of Billie Holiday's childhood, the father fades in and out of focus, an oddly discarnate presence. Charles Senior may have been an unfortunate role model for his son: itinerant entertainer, suddenly (and vexingly) present or suddenly (and mysteriously) absent. In most accounts, it's Parker's steely Baptist mother who dominates: if Charles Jr had a better than average childhood, it was down to Addie Parker, who toiled hard and made his future the focus of her life. None of the books pries very far under this bright but somewhat inert picture. The near suffocating attention Addie lavished on Charlie feels not entirely healthy: maybe not the full Oedipal, but definitely on the doorstep. Routes around limited space, humid closeness, proxy mates: one exiled Charles and his over-adored replacement. When Charlie brings his young wife, Rebecca, onto the scene, she and Mama Parker merge into one edgeless figure, set up to tend his majesty's regally unpredictable needs 24/7. (It's perhaps no surprise he grew into a man with such little impulse control.) At one point in *Kansas City Lightning: The Rise and Times of Charlie Parker*, Stanley Crouch describes Mrs Parker's attitude to Rebecca as that towards an 'interloper'; otherwise, no one embellishes this score with any oblique psychoanalytic riffs. (Oh, for a quick burst of Melanie Klein!) There's a muggy feeling of various unexamined ellipses, lacunae. The most obvious tranquillized elephant in the room: if things were so cosy, how to explain Charlie's greedy embrace of pain-killing drugs at just this point? A few weak shots of morphine administered after a car crash are nominated the fatal glass of beer; Chuck Haddix, in *Bird*, then has a visiting GP suddenly burst into dark warnings about the hell-broth of addiction. This seems a tad unlikely. (According to Haddix, the doc warns that as an addict Charlie will have – at best – twenty years left. Twenty years! To a young black man in that time and place, two decades of intermittent bliss hardly counts as the sternest counsel imaginable.) If Haddix seems lost in some creaky 1930s melodrama about the evils of narcomania, Crouch has a whole palette of gory details regarding sexual organs, soiled bandages, abortion and afterbirth, which sits very oddly indeed with his general professorial demeanour. It's as if both writers had caught Birditis by osmosis: everything feels simultaneously too close, but strangely unreal. Nothing quite coheres. (Also: why towards the end of his life did Parker become quite so obsessed with not being buried in his and his beloved Mama's hometown?)

Charles Jr had a typical spoiled child's approach to new enthusiasms: taking them up and putting them down, not ready for the slow circular grind of daily practice. Two years passed without any signs of extraordinary musical aptitude; as Giddins has it, only young Charlie's 'obsessiveness begged notice'. Then the sonic gyroscope seems to shift inside: he digs in, locates somewhere to play from, aim towards. Finally settled on the alto sax, Parker put in the required slog. The same pattern on the bandstand or off, learning his instrument or injecting drugs: long idle hours of dust and scratch and empty mind; and then this sudden click of magic acceleration, curling overflow. Gnarly young apprentice Charlie slowly takes on the shiny lineaments of mythical Bird. (The nickname was a combined tribute to Parker's outsized appetite and his far-sightedness. A literal on-the-road incident: speeding to a country gig, the car Parker was in ran over some farmer's 'yardbird'. Everyone else in the car saw dead poultry; Parker, always one thought ahead, saw that night's chicken in the pot.)

Initially, Parker would have played for an almost exclusively black audience: for other musicians, at so-called 'cutting contests' and long after-hours jams; or for Friday and Saturday night crowds who appreciated flair and artistry but most of all came for the big weekend get-down catharsis. Crouch gives the best account here of the jazz bands of the 1940s: how they played together, changed the air in the room, rose up as one through dancing bodies. This was the soil Parker thrived in: any ode to his improvising genius has to acknowledge the galvanizing friction of all those he played with and learned from. Many contemporaries revered the young upstart for his bandstand technique, but resented him personally: the jive and murk of his life brought jazz back down again to the myth of an elementally untidy black life, the same old tale of two sides of the river and the bad side of town, the need to explain things all over again from scratch when it was way past time to have to crank out such tired footnotes – jazz isn't a silly gimmick, we are artists, we are professionals. Parker – the king of id – refused to acknowledge any real boundary between private impulse and public decorum; his discomfiting and unpredictable behaviour even got him banned from Birdland, the New York club ostensibly named in his honour.

You maybe catch a faint echo of that exasperated tone from Parker's biographers, too, as they try to explain just why jazz was once such a huge, and hugely catalysing, part of public discourse in America. Haddix makes bafflingly large claims for his own work ('Separating the man from the myth has proved to be an elusive effort for those who have written about Charlie – until now'), but has no real surprises or new slants in store; his is a sturdy, unexceptionable, journeyman study. *Celebrating Bird* is a revised edition of a book that originally came out in 1987, and is the one I'd recommend for curious outsiders. Giddins does the best job of explaining Parker on a technical level, what it was he did to earn his reputation as a peerless innovator: the tensile 'logic and coherence' behind what might seem to outsiders like 'an explosion of sound, a scramble, an incomprehensible provocation'. How he worked a breathing space deep inside old riffs and drowsy songs, prising apart tired chord arrangements and fanning them out round the waiting night in kaleidoscopic new variations. Parker's tone on the alto sax was clipped, light, skittering – actually more like solo piano than other saxophone players of the time. (You can definitely hear the hours he spent listening to the blind keyboard maestro Art Tatum. Can we also hear echoes of his father's tap dance and later clickety-clack train-bound times? It seems an obvious thought but no one raises it.)

Even during his lifetime, jazz fans were obsessed with Parker in a way they simply weren't with other, equally gifted players. On-the-hoof Boswells trailed Parker from club to club with clunky reel-to-reel equipment, back when it was like carrying a circus clown's car on one shoulder of your baggy suit. Giddins makes a stab at totting up the figures: 'More than 350 Parker improvisations recorded privately between 1947 and 1954, excluding posthumously discovered studio performances, surfaced in the thirty years after his death.' But he's already erased that figure by the bottom of the page. In a revised footnote he reckons the initial estimate conservative: uber-fan Dean Benedetti alone, in the year 1947-48, collected more than seven hours of Parker solos and snippets. Monomania like this can be hard for outsiders to process. Isn't this obsession with technique alone a bit lopsided, a bit inhuman? What about emotional sway? I'd have liked one of these true believers to argue Parker's case more, rather than take it as given that his was an irresistible magic. I love Parker's music, but it's not what I'd choose to smooth anyone into jazz appreciation. It can seem hard-shelled, intransigent. (The two words of true-believer praise that crop up most are 'virtuosity' and 'velocity'.) If you did have to play devil's advocate, the brief might go: for all his technical verve and power, Parker's is a limited palette; his playing, while breathtaking, rarely admits softer moods or qualities – anything of drift, reflection, loss. The one time he instigated a more calmly interpretative project – 1950's *Bird with Strings* – it was not an unqualified success. Parker's impatient stiletto tone guts the delicate membrane of his chosen mainstream standards; it doesn't sound as if he is interpreting these popular songs so much as assailing them, giving them a hard time to see if they pass muster.

It may not be coincidental that the one performance many people cite as Parker's most moving is one he himself disowned. I was stunned when I first heard 'Lover Man' on Volume 1 of the Dial collection – this really is art that leaves you nowhere to hide. You might say it's the one time his life and art roughly coincided – where you can read one through the other. A recording session had been booked, but Parker was out of heroin, and drinking heavily to numb the pain. A healthy (i.e. heroin-soaked) Parker might have breezed through 'Lover Man', playing abstruse games with all the harmonic underpinnings, half-mocking its sentimentality, exposing all the song's rubbery bones. Instead, he's audibly out of sorts: you can hear how much it costs him to summon the breath to make it through to the end. This is an unbuttoned rendition you either find unbearably moving (while noting that this close to collapse Parker's sense of artistry still kicks in); or you think, as Parker did, that it should never have been made public. (He was reportedly furious with Russell for releasing it.) I don't think our only response to 'Lover Man' has to be a meanly voyeuristic one. It may be a cracked whisper rather than his usual keening flight, it may have come from a pitiful, blasted place, but it sounds like a last desperate attempt at communication, before the lights go out.

One of the problems with trying to profile Parker may be that everything is already upfront, undisguised, heaped up in a monstrously untidy pile. Parker wasn't one to tiptoe through the realm of the senses; there was very little interfering static between his having a lurid idea and making it happen. Any biographer used to sieving through decorous public behaviour for dark and hidden motifs might well exclaim (as someone once did of Max Beerbohm): 'For God's sake, take off your face and reveal the mask underneath.' It leaves the biographer with the unfamiliar project of clothing their subject, not stripping them bare. Which is not necessarily a bad thing with a life like Parker's, which can feel over-itemized: it might force the writer to come up with deeper, odder, more illuminating personal responses.

In 1981, Stanley Crouch started interviewing people who'd known and played with Parker; 32 years (and a MacArthur 'genius' grant) later, *Kansas City Lightning* represents the fruit of all his obsessive research. Well, kind of, as it turns out that this is only the first half of Crouch's long-anticipated study: by the end of its 334 pages Parker has just turned 21, and all the most celebrated music and more infamous Life of Bird stuff is still to come. Crouch builds up a steady, rising momentum and then – dead air. Halfway through the premiere of some brazen new polyphonic suite, the band leader brings his hands down, draws a halt and marches offstage. Crouch has always been a contrarian, but his decision to break off the story this way seems notably odd – especially as you'd think Parker's curt, fiery life had a pretty singular integral arc. (Who knows what psychological horse-trading, and/or grim publishing politics were involved in this decision, but it now looks like Crouch will spend more time on this biography than Parker himself spent on earth.) Also, some kind of drag kicked in for me about two-thirds of the way through: I hit a wall and had real trouble getting back into Crouch's expansive, carbo-bulked step. In smaller portions, Crouch dazzles; as a whole night's mezze, the text feels just a bit too rich, dense, self-delightedly overcooked. It confirms a prior feeling that Crouch is at his best in the short-jab arena of essay, polemic, reply.

When Clint Eastwood's 1988 biopic *Bird* came out,

Crouch wrote a piece ('Birdland: Clint Eastwood, Charlie Parker and America') which wasn't just critical of this or that detail: it felt more like an attempt to unmake the film, to deny Eastwood (or any white person) the right to make such a film. (I thought the essay fundamentally wrongheaded, but as rhetoric it was unputdownable; his 2006 collection, *Considering Genius*, containing essay-length appreciations of Miles, Mingus, Ellington et al, is essential reading.) Many people in jazz see Crouch as a kind of rebop Christopher Hitchens – an ex-Free Jazz maven who blimped out and has become more and more inflexibly conservative with time. Big Poppa with the rod of correction, dismissing whole swathes of new work, cleaving instead to dependable figures like the trumpeter Wynton Marsalis. (I'm not enough of a buff to judge someone like Marsalis in Crouchian terms – he has a deeply felt and interiorized sense of the music's history, theory and technique – but on instinct alone I'm baffled: even at his best Marsalis seems like an exemplary but perfectly lifeless simulacrum or museum piece.) Crouch wants to explain where Parker came from in order to reclaim where jazz subsequently went: a way to underline his own – some would say perilously nostalgic – vision of what jazz always was, and should always remain. Through Parker he can celebrate the majesty and integrity of certain black cultural traditions – most of all, the ESP itch and summons of big band improvisation-within-bounds. And it has to be said, the first half of *Kansas City Lightning* is a flat-out joy and revelation: in the sections that deal with bandleaders, Saturday nights out, food, clothes, seduction, argument, Crouch's prose catches fire. He's winningly suasive on the whys and wherefores of the era; the only problem may be that he is far more memorable on the 'times' of this great pre-war moment than he is on Parker's own singular 'rise'. You look around for Bird, and he's gone. You can just detect a small splash of exit at the far edge of Crouch's frame.

In December 1945, Parker, Dizzy Gillespie and others took a train west for a big club date. Stopped in Chicago overnight, they took the chance to jam with some local musicians and missed their morning connection on the sleek Santa Fe *Chief*; they ended up on a far slower mail train, stretching the two-day trip out to nearly a week. Idling at a tiny depot in the middle of the Nevada desert, Dizzy looked out the window only to see Bird staggering off on foot across the endless empty plains, his battered saxophone case under his arm. He was sick, and trying to score.

Haddix gives a nice account of this tale (originally related by Ross Russell), and it's one of the few times here you get any sense of air, space, American horizons, a world beyond the shades-drawn jazz life. Time measured out in spoons and bottle-tops, in stale boarding-house bedrooms and tiny clubs, in street corner telephone kiosks. In *Bird Lives!* Russell has Parker conducting half his life in taxi cabs: he hid out in their back seats to swallow pills, write music, consummate relationships, sleep; held on to them for entire days, as combination office, waiting room and bedroom. Even at rest, Parker keeps moving. He would nod out on the bandstand then snap to, pulling ferociously inventive lines up from the seabed of near coma. In the long run, such all-or-nothing logic exacts a heavy toll: physical enervation first, but one's emotional/intellectual life can also take a protracted beating. It's hardly conducive to any kind of art that might grow and deepen over a lifetime. You develop certain muscles at the expense of others. You don't work out how to pace yourself. You do not, in Ishmael Reed's radiant words, learn how to fall. You become rooted, boxed in, inflexible. Even when Parker went abroad, he didn't soak up any new influences. Miles went to France and learned to speak existentialist, fell hard for Juliette Greco, was awakened to African textures, checked out Picasso. Bird went to France and cottoned on to a Belgian bebop fanatic and (uh oh) pharmacist, who liked to befriend the premier league of US jazz addicts. He had a whole room full of pure legal narcotics: a dark rainbow of graded heroin from Marseille, Naples, Beirut, Seoul, Istanbul, pure pharmaceutical morphine from Basel. For two weeks, Bird had the strung-out time of his life, curled up inside this nest of thorns.

In truth, it's hard to see where Parker might have landed next, if he hadn't exited when he did; there's a melancholy feeling of peaks already scaled, with only decline or repetition ahead. He was well on the way to being the jazz equivalent of a punchy old boxer, someone the up-and-comers use to train with, before moving on. Deprived of heroin, all Bird's Grimm-paw prickliness could return with shocking force. In 1955, following an especially sad, disordered set with Parker and the equally troubled Bud Powell, the young bass magus Charles Mingus dragged up to the microphone and apologized to the audience. 'Ladies and gentlemen, please don't associate me with any of this. This is not jazz. These are sick people.'

There came a point when Birdland closed its doors, 52nd Street emptied. (There were political manoeuvrings behind the hey-daddyo jive: worries about returning servicemen having way too good a time in *those* sorts of club.) In the jazz world, things were changing too. Broad-cloth bebop suits already seemed a bit clownish. Some players still drew on bop's harsh, stuttering example, but many more didn't. Some lit out for a slower, more reflective path, a music of languid West Coast breeze: limpid, crystalline, Pacific blue. Miles was looking inward, and also networking: his sharp clothes, measured contempt, subtle fire, appealed to a younger, hipper crowd. None of these developments could have been plotted from Bird's example, and none suited his particular sensibility. He was 34. There are heights of success which feel like a very personal form of failure.

Ross Russell still gives the best – the most distressing – picture of Bird's final weeks and months. 'His movements were mechanical, erratic, purposeless. They followed a mindless pattern of disorder and whim. High life had become low life.' He spent whole nights riding the subway alone. He talked incessantly about death, leaping into the river. He was sick now, deep down in his peculiar sense of time; the old sure feel for currents and vectors, exits and hideaways, had fallen away. He was out of time. He zigzags through rainy New York, drinking port wine behind the dead windows of abandoned buildings: a nest fashioned from ulcers, debt, old reeds, blood. He's never felt such a bitter taste in his mouth before. A rough bird, jet black, alights on his hand. He recalls an old golden song, from long ago. 'Goin' to Kansas City, sorry that I can't take you.'

There is one way of looking at Parker that none of these books touches, which is that the arc of his success also measured the extent of his failure and fall: he went too far, too fast, in one solitary direction, leaving himself no outs, alternatives, breathing space. (Yves Bonnefoy: 'Love perfection because it is the threshold / But deny it once known, once dead forget it / Imperfection is the summit.') Maybe the reason we're still drawn to Parker's oblique, messy outline is that he wasn't any kind of seamless paragon: it was never brilliant technique that was the lure, but the imperfect, unreadable man. For all their careful, respectful merits, a few weeks after finishing these books I could barely call up a single memorable detail, whereas I can still bring to mind whole sections of Russell's much disparaged Life of Bird. (Not for nothing, but once you get past the pimp-face stare-down, Miles's autobiography is also effortlessly illuminating on Parker's personal toughness and nonpareil musical technique. He gives us a Bird who's a painter in sound, a Picasso of syncopation: a beady-eared Cubist playing four versions of a tune at once.) Russell's account – dodgy though some of its anecdotal evidence may be – feels like it was written in a rush of genuine excitement. It's not pretty, but Parker is a genuine presence in the room: sweaty, sulky, delicate; brutal, playful, paradoxical. Half-flesh, half-feather: carnal daemon, weightless changeling.

I keep returning to all the different images: sometimes I think we might discern more of the true story here, if we blur our eyes and dream a little. All the photos, but also certain uncanny paintings by Jean-Michel Basquiat and Beauford Delaney. Like this lovely photo from 1940: avid young Charles, barely twenty, with a great big springtime smile on his face, pointing to someone or something just out of frame: a bebop presidential candidate, working the hustings. The first few times I glanced at it, I didn't really see: it's actually Bird having fun inside a Kansas City photo booth, and the someone or something he's pointing at with such unabashed glee is himself. He's finally found someone he

can't fleece or best or seduce – and, it appears, it's only
made him all the happier.

SWOONATRA:
THE AFTERLIVES OF FRANK SINATRA

Reveille with Beverly is a now largely forgotten 1943 film
starring Ann Miller and the great Franklin Pangborn.
Worked up from an equally forgotten US radio series
it's a corny but percipient tale about a spunky young DJ
who's hep to the vital Swing rhythm the kids all dig, and
the stuffy station owner who wants no part of her inde-
corous jive. Miller, as the wide-awake DJ, specializes in
the wake-up call requests of local servicemen, and the
film was a big hit with US military personnel stationed
overseas during the Second World War: 'Gooood morning, Potsdam!' Forgotten it may be, but *Reveille* has one
of the all-time great soundtracks: Count Basie, Duke
Ellington, proto rock'n'roller Ella Mae Morse doing
'Cow Cow Boogie', and, in his Hollywood debut, a slen-
der young reed called Frank Sinatra.

Even at the time, Sinatra's cameo didn't cause much of
a stir, and *Reveille* doesn't feature in many official filmog-
raphies; but it did mark, in its modest way, the inception
of Sinatra's solo career. He had just left the Tommy
Dorsey band, had a slick new press agent called Milton
Rubin, and the beginnings of what we would now call
a posse. It was a personal turning point for the young
man Jimmy Durante dubbed 'Moonlight Sinatra', at a
moment when bigger changes were in the air. This was
an era when audiences bugged out to live music, rather
than losing themselves in recorded sound. Vocalists had
little real power: they were smiley, yes-sir emblems over
the arch of touring big bands. But a hesitant jockeying
for power had started up among band leaders, singers,
agents and arrangers, and what came next would surprise nearly everyone.

When Sinatra's new booking agency, GAC, persuaded the owners of New York's Paramount Theatre to add him to its big New Year show, their driven young client had none of the star power of already signed performers like Benny Goodman and Peggy Lee; his billing read 'Extra Added Attraction', and for Sinatra this particular gig was a pretty big deal. As Donald Clarke puts it in *All or Nothing at All: A Life of Frank Sinatra* (1997), the Paramount Theatre was 'one of the shrines of the Swing era'. And so, on 30 December 1942, Sinatra was brought onstage, in an almost desultory way, by Benny Goodman. 'And now, Frank Sinatra...' The 27-year-old Francis Albert Sinatra stepped up, and history turned a small corner. He was met by a tsunami of hysterical screams from a passel of young female fans. Goodman was initially thrown, completely struck dumb in fact, then looked over his shoulder and blurted out: 'What the fuck is that?' Clarke: 'Sinatra laughed, and his fear left him.'

Sinatra may have left damp seats and shredded hankies in his skinny-bod wake but he was nobody's idea of a teenager. By the time of the Paramount 'Swoonatra' incident he was four years married to his first wife, Nancy, with one young child (Nancy Jr) and a second (Frank Jr) just about to arrive. He dressed like other adults of the time. (His sole concession to dandyism was a lasciviously Borromean, outsize bow-tie.) His day-to-day social intercourse was conducted among hard-bitten, resourcefully cynical musicians – we can just imagine the ribbings they dished out to young Francis about his undiscerning new fan base. Sinatra's bandmates were actually more bewildered than bothered by this latest development: despite his major rep as a real ladies' man, no one had him pegged as the next Valentino. This was a scrawny, underfed-looking Italian kid with big ears: there was definitely something of a semolina dough Mickey Mouse about his looks. But he obviously gave off some subtle radar peep of rapt carnality, equal parts vulnerable boy-child and lazily virile roué. Unlike the pendulum-hipped Presleys up ahead, he could intimate sexual confidence with his eyes alone. His sexual charge was like his song: underplayed, tinged with unflappable cool picked up second-hand in the shady cloisters of jazz. Just as he could mine exquisite sadness from superficially happy songs, he managed to suggest bedtime fevers with a barely perceptible finger's brush of his microphone stand.

As Clarke points out, none of this was entirely new: there had been previous scenes of clammy hysteria triggered by male musicians and screen stars, from Franz Liszt to Rudy Vallée. But these hormonal crazes tended to fizzle out, often ignominiously, even if (like Sinatra) you had a resourceful press agent hyping the script. This was a watershed moment between the insider hegemony of jazz-inflected Swing and the wider plains of Elvis-era pop music. The 'Swoonatra' craze might easily have been a barrier to wider public acceptance for Sinatra, but as it transpired he made the coming decade entirely his own. In conventional sales-ledger terms it was his starry apotheosis.

Working the road in the 1930s and 1940s with the Harry James and Tommy Dorsey bands, Sinatra acquired a lot of jazz life knowledge by osmosis. (Jazz inflections peppered his speech for the rest of his life: 'I've known discouragement, despair and all those other cats.') He learned what not to do: how to hold back, live in the space between instrumental arcs. By Sinatra's own account, the three main figures who shaped his navigation of song – how to float and sustain and linger – were Tommy Dorsey ('the General Motors of the band business'), Billie Holiday and Bing Crosby. Anyone surprised by the inclusion of the latter should do a bit of digging: Crosby is a fascinating character. As well as a subtly revolutionary singer he was a technophile obsessed with recording techniques, and with how best to refine and update them to suit the new, softer style of singing and playing. Crosby was the original 'crooner' when the world was full of vocalists who belted out songs to the back of the hall. An old-school jazz fan like Sinatra, he worshipped Louis Armstrong and closely studied Satchmo's self-presentation and singular way with a tune. Crosby's delivery was 'cool' in a way that was entirely new to the mainstream, studded with jazz tics such as unexpected pauses and slurred or flattened notes. His understanding of microphone technique meant he could step back and let the audience come to him. He was a pivotal figure on the journey of cool jazz tones from a largely black, underground world into the mainstream, and a big influence on younger acts like Sinatra.

In the 1998 Arena documentary *The Voice of the Century*, Sinatra talks about how he first learned to sing by listening to horn players 'and how they breathe', the way certain jazz musicians can make us feel a melody as something both impossibly fragile and finally unbreakable. He mentions Tommy Dorsey again ('I may be the only singer who ever took vocal lessons from a trombone'), and Ben Webster (one of the first acts showcased on Sinatra's own Reprise label). But a third influence is more notable, and an indication of just how deeply jazz was lodged in the young singer's soul: the tenor saxophonist Lester Young. Young was Billie Holiday's musical other half, a quiet innovator and, ultimately, a rather tragic figure. In life and music the dandyish Young pushed softly against the macho grain: he could be dainty, impossibly sweet and tender, almost defenceless. His musical tone was airy, elusive, a musical braille. Towards the end of his life, so the story goes, 'Prez' (as Holiday dubbed him) would sit in his cheap hotel room and robotically drink and stare out into the New York air and play Sinatra records over and over again.

The young Sinatra certainly imbibed much from the jazz-world exemplars of Cool, but perhaps we can also hear the influence of another quasi-masonic clique, one Sinatra's name was often linked with. Consider the following, from *Cosa Nostra* (2004), John Dickie's history of the Sicilian Mafia: 'Anyone who was worthy of being described as mafioso therefore had a certain something, an attribute called "mafia". "Cool" is about the closest modern English equivalent.' Discourse among 'men of honour' was all about 'great reserve, the things that are not said'. They communicated in 'code, hints, fragments of phrases, stony stares, significant silences'. What this definition of 'mafia' suggests is almost a kind of illicit soulfulness. The rock'n'roll era's new decadents may have crashed expensive rides into pools and used TV sets for drunken target practice, but Sinatra's offstage associations spoke of an altogether more serious class of transgression. He hung out, it was whispered, with real adepts of dark illegality: Murder, as the phrase had it, Incorporated. This was likely a dream come true twice over for the young Hoboken kid who looked up to iron-willed 'men of honour' and admired professionals of every stripe, from whiskey-bar waiters to world statesmen. (Sinatra was always a devil for the small-print detail of how jobs got done.) Here was the quasi-mythic

Sinatra of a thousand headlines to come: a figure who commingled gentle songs of heartache with rumours of drunken vulgarity and unspeakable violence. It's debatable how much harm the Mafia rumours did to his public image in the long run. For some fans, it was an undeniable (if ethically troublesome) lure that lent his music a kind of infernal gravitas. Some association with Mafia guys was probably all but unavoidable, given their omnipresence on the live music scene: the clubs they owned, the quid pro quo favours they expected.

The Mafia connection had relatively little exposure early on, but the gossip-column sorority had plenty of other tut-tut material to expose: his flagrant extra-marital promiscuity; an often ill-advisedly haughty attitude to what was not yet termed the media; and a rather too convenient, for some, 4F status which exempted him from action in the Second World War. OK, he did have a punctured eardrum. But 'psychoneurosis'? (Sample headline: 'Is Crooning Essential?') He was given a lot of grief for being adult in ways that didn't accord with the party line drawn up by the era's self-appointed moral arbiters. They wanted: a politically neutral homebody and popular music puppet. He proffered: a volatile, sleep-around, finger-pointing Democrat. Much of the press antagonism also involved more or less sub rosa forms of racism and class-based snobbery. A largely middle-class, faux-genteel, WASP-ish media was never going to take this working-class, Italian Catholic, faux wiseguy at his own estimation. Anyone who thinks there has never been a subtly hierarchical class system in America might consider lines such as the following, quoted by Kitty Kelley in her 1986 no-turn-left-unstoned Sinatra biography/exposé, *His Way*. In 1943, a writer for the *New Republic* wrote of Sinatra's

Paramount coup: 'Nearly all the bobby-soxers whom I saw ... gave every appearance of being children of the poor.' E.J. Kahn Jr, writing in the *New Yorker*, added his five cents' worth: 'Most of his fans are plain, lonely girls from lower-middle-class homes.' Kelley herself occasionally sounds just the tiniest bit snippy: 'Through marriage, the Sinatras had elevated themselves socially, so there were few traces left of the showgirl in a feathered headdress ... or the saloon singer with the grade school education.' Material aspiration may be the very hub and hothouse of the American Dream – just don't aspire too high or you might embarrass yourself. You get the distinct feeling Kelley disapproves of Sinatra's fourth wife, Barbara, because she insisted on giving millions rather than thousands to certain charities, such as a programme for sexually abused children. A lose-lose situation: keep your money to yourself and you're pilloried as the unfeeling rich; spend all your time working for the less fortunate and you're caricatured as one of the brittle porcelain-doll Ladies Who Charity Lunch.

Kelley also quotes a 1979 *Washington Star* editorial on Sinatra, dizzy with its own mock perplexity: 'That such beautiful music should emerge from such vulgarity is one of the great mysteries of the age.' Again, just a hint of class sneer: how dare this nouveau riche non-Wasp possess a working soul! It's important to keep in mind that he was only one generation removed from Ellis Island: Sinatra's father arrived from Sicily in 1903. One version of the origins of the slur 'wop' figures it as an Ellis Island acronym: With Out Papers. (This is now disputed by etymologists, but even as apocrypha seems telling.) In the early 1960s, a lot of the onstage humour Sinatra indulged in with his Rat Pack buddies exploited a kind of third-drink *détournement* of such racial epithets.

Why, there was manly solidarity in mutual ribbing! We got something like a rainbow coalition here! Two wops, a nigger kike, a Polack and a token Wasp! The most convincing take on this touchy matter is provided by Sinatra's long-time (African-American) valet, George Jacobs. In his immensely entertaining memoir *Mr S: The Last Word on Frank Sinatra* (2003), he defends Sinatra and the other Rat Pack roustabouts, and says the only people he ever got a real nasty sizzle of racism from were a few Mafia bosses, and the dependably unpleasant monster-patriarch Joseph P. Kennedy. Jacobs paraphrases the Rat Pack's foreign minister without portfolio, Dean Martin: 'Wops, nigs, hebes, what the fuck was the difference? We were all up against the wall and fucking well better stick together.'

As with Elvis Presley and Charlie Parker, you feel Destiny's real leg-up was provided by the ferocious will of Sinatra's mother. Most people seem to have regarded Dolly as the real man about the house: Sinatra's father, Marty, an easy-going ghost, barely registers in most biographies. As an Italian-Catholic working-class woman, Dolly Sinatra née Natalina Garaventa had innumerable counts against her. Yet by fair means or foul, she charmed and blustered and backhanded her way through until she was as near to a female version of a 'man of honour' as made no difference. Dissatisfied with the doll's house limitations of conventional wifely behaviour, she successfully hijacked the rough, violent and Irish-dominated world of local Democratic politics. She also dabbled on the side as the local Hoboken abortionist. First Dolly, then Ava Gardner – his second wife, genuinely wild, guiltlessly Dionysian – overshadowed, shaped and furrowed Sinatra's life. Similarly boozy, foul-mouthed and wilful, Ava and Dolly got on like a hen-house on fire. Dolly was one helluva guy's guy's doll; just as her precious only child could often present as an oddly haunted and feminine guy: as much as he was undoubtedly the big boss man of myth, he could also be prissy, neurotic, remote. Even into late middle age, even for his closest buddies, carousing with Sinatra was a serious three-line whip: beg off early, fall asleep, order a coffee instead of Jack Daniel's, and you risked expulsion, exile, the Antarctica of his disaffection. He could not abide the ends of days: it was one thing he had no control over. So he made an enemy of the clock, of merely human time, each night's feeble apocalypse: that dire moment when the ring-a-ding bell must be wrapped in cotton wool and stowed away. Then came the risky, occluded territory of sleep. Sinatra seems to have shared a pathology with Kingsley Amis: a fear of the shadows at the end of the night-time tunnel. What was hiding there he was so reluctant to explore?

Sinatra had none of the nice-and-easy-does-it spirit of his pal Dean Martin. He was also deathly serious about his craft. That may ultimately be what differentiates him from more than capable contemporaries like Tony Bennett and Mel Tormé: with Sinatra there's less obvious technique on show and more personality. Except, what is most characteristic about that personality is how unshowy it is: how it often feels deeply submerged, and hard to touch. He can sound on the edge of something trance-like, 'lost in a dream'. Our favourite singers often have some scintillant flaw or uniquely cracked marker: hints of an old accent poking through; sudden unpredictable breaks in the calm, confident voice; cynicism interlaced with giggly childlike joy. You hear nothing like this in Sinatra: at times his song is closer to a kind of resplendent anonymity; he never makes things too obvious, italicizing what he thinks the listener ought to be feeling. It's notable for its lack of conspicuous drama, the antipodean opposite of today's showboaty *X Factor* model.

Sinatra Sings Great Songs from Great Britain (1962) isn't one of the more celebrated Sinatra collections, but it's a tribute to how the music business operated in that era that something knocked out in three days sounds the way it does: note-perfect, rococo, panoramic. Today, such a project would gobble up egos, itineraries and budgets. (The year 1962 saw the release of six new Sinatra long players. This seems inconceivable now, but was not far removed from the contemporary norm.) Sinatra may have riled a whole army of newspaper columnists with his wise-guy intransigence and superstar ways, but when it came to certain matters he was all business. One of the extras inside the sumptuous new box set, *Sinatra: London*, is a lovely fold-out photo of Sinatra at work in the CTS Bayswater studios in June 1962: 360 degrees of hard-nosed session guys, flawless casual wear, high-tar cigarettes, music stands. The hard work of Easy Listening.

Sinatra opens his British sortie with a familiar move: just his supple, unaccompanied voice stating the main refrain. Here it's 'The Very Thought of You', but he'd pulled the same trick the year before with the line 'Never thought I'd fall' in 'I'm Getting Sentimental over You', which opened the memoir-in-sound *I Remember Tommy*. Listen to how he strings out the word 'ordinary' in the line 'the little ordinary things', thereby making it far from ordinary. Then with the line 'the mere idea of you' he draws out the word 'mere' as though it were the sweetest qualifier in the world: dissolving 'mere' into 'idea' he makes the very idea of 'mere' sound transcendent. It is subtly erotic and boldly unshowy. It calls to mind another such moment in the song 'It Was a Very Good Year' (1966): when he sings 'with all that perfumed hair, and it came undone' he stretches out the word 'came' into an arc and tumble of rapture, so that it feels as if the word itself has been unzipped, and is about to fall undone.

Elsewhere on *GB*, Sinatra manages the unthinkable and pulls us happily into the shallows of that doughty standard 'We'll Meet Again'. To redeem something stultifyingly over-familiar: this is the acme of interpretative singing. Sinatra takes soiled £5 words and makes them glisten like mystic opals, his voice like spring light clarifying a dusty catacomb. One slice of the *Sinatra: London* box set is a Frankophile's delight: a separate CD comprised of outtakes from the studio sessions for *GB*. Sinatra is relaxed, polite, perfectionist. 'Hold it, hold it. May we please do an inter-cut from bar 55?' Whatever the aural equivalent of 'hawk-eyed' is, here is a peerless example.

When Sinatra says 'Great Britain' he means London, and for London read a certain stratum of high society – the kind of fine gin fizz evenings that end with Princess Margaret at the Steinway. Sinatra's Great Britain is an Impressionist painting in sound: a mise-en-song of dawn and dew, lanes and lawns; nightingales doing their solo act in rain-iced gardens; autumn among indecisive leaves. Firelight glows and magic is abroad. Angels have reservations at the Ritz. 'The hush of the silver dew,' he sings, sounding hushed and dewy. Strings shiver and slide.

Sinatra was one of the first musicians to see the long-playing album as an opportunity for sustained mood music: a pocket of time focused entirely on one defining concept or tone; a quasi-cinematic reverie for listeners to sink into and dream along with. You could make a case for Sinatra as one of the original 'ambient music' theorists, mixing up discrete tones into one balmy cocktail. For the music business the switch from live music to recorded in the 1950s was as much of a revolution as Hollywood's changeover from silent cinema to the talkies. A singer bellowing before a big band on stage was one kind of music; Sinatra and one of his favoured arrangers piecing together polyvalent tone poetry was something else altogether. It's no coincidence that so much music from the next decade sounded so good, and still does, half a century on. At this make-or-break point, many jazz-schooled musicians saw which way was up and swapped the marriage-destroying purgatory of touring for well-remunerated union-protected session work. This meant you might find the same artfully capable background players on a Sinatra album, a Phil Spector 45 and a Brian Wilson pop suite, as well as anything from supper-club Soul to Exploitation soundtracks and misty Exotica. The Second World War had also worked a kind of happy miscegenation into America's alienated micro-cultures: people from different backgrounds met in the services and found they liked each other's homegrown musics. (After the war the 'hillbilly' Chet Baker ended up playing cool West Coast jazz, while Miles Davis huddled with Gil Evans and exulted in European melancholy.) Air travel became cheaper and more widely available, and Sinatra slipped easily into the role of poet laureate of the new global leisure; think of all those great songs celebrating aeroplane take-offs and spicy foreign affairs, flighty fun in foreign places.

Using the two-sided forty-minute album, Sinatra began to spin his needle around a compass of different themes: travel of course (*Come Fly with Me*, 1958), time and mortality (*September of My Years*, 1965), inner/outer space (*Moonlight Sinatra*, 1966), and most of all, romance and its discontents. In lonely-guy collations like *In the Wee Small Hours* (1955), *Sings Songs for Only the Lonely* (1958) and (my personal favourite) *No One Cares* (1959), he makes wilting neurasthenia seem like the height of enviable urban glamour. You want to be this white-gabardined, sad-eyed figure: a lovelorn cipher nestled among loveless shadows, crying into his shot glass, sighing under impervious stars. You want to tarry inside the ports of call on the album sleeves: wood-panelled saloon bar, modern apartment, skyscraper's embrace. And, behind the endless itinerary of glamorous jet-set destinations, the key topography at the heart of it all: the space of recording itself.

It's maybe no coincidence that Sinatra's take on the torch song aesthetic occurs at precisely this postwar moment. The rise in sales of long-playing albums and the idea of entertaining 'at home' made perfect sense in the buoyant Eisenhower economy. As Peter J. Levinson puts it in *September in the Rain* (2001), his useful biography of Sinatra's arranger, Nelson Riddle: 'It was the decade of the suburban house, the six o'clock cocktail shaker and the regulation grey flannel suit... Beautiful love songs served up with lush string backgrounds perfectly reflected the quiet and serenity of the decade.' Global conflagration was over and people turned inward. There's an implicit edge to the idea of 'home' on Sinatra's torch song trilogy: this is no longer a small-town white-picket fort, the family at the heart of the community; this is a big city hangout, a coldly seductive swinger's pad. You've just moved to the busy and populous city, but feel more lonely than ever. 'Uneasy, in my easy chair...' The core paradox of much Easy Listening from the 1950s and 1960s: it was often a pendant to very un-easy, asocial states of mind.

The sleeve for the UK edition of *In The Wee Small Hours* (1955) provides an interior snapshot of an era, a line-up of allegorical consumer objects. At the centre of the front-room still life is a stately radiogram, anticipating our own scene of listening. A thick onyx ashtray, already lined with butts. A clear Pyrex cup. (Cappuccino tonight, not booze: insomnia not blissfully sloppy blackout.) Art Deco clock, reading somewhere around 2.39 a.m. *LIFE* magazine with a Marilyn cover. Selection of shiny LP sleeves scattered over the rug. Best of all – there among them is the original US sleeve of *In the Wee Small Hours*! All these hallowed objects add up to something like an Eisenhower-era retouch of Dürer's *Melancholia*: alchemical union under the cold urban stars.

The songs on *In the Wee Small Hours* flicker and return, time and again, to figures of sleep, dream, waking, hallucination. 'Deep in a dream of you ... The smoke makes a stairway ... I wake with a start ... I close my eyes and there you are ...' The threshold state of torch: a strange mixture of wooziness and clarity, scepticism and passivity. The prickly valetudinarian ache of the torch singer, forever taking their own pulse. For all that the torch mood – especially in Sinatra's habitual rendering – is associated with enthusiastic drink-downing, I've always thought the mood was far more opium pipe reverie than another round of boilermakers. 'Shadows gathered in the air...' In his pioneering study *Elevator Music* (1994), Joseph Lanza writes perceptively of Nelson Riddle's work and how a 'standard Easy Listening formula' frequently gives way to something far more uncanny, even sinister. 'This is music in suspension where drowning is only a sensual slumber... songs of time travel into amniotic bliss.' Riddle was adept at complementing moony or upbeat material with barely detectable and often deeply unnerving bittersweet undertones. His note-perfect arrangement of *In the Wee Small Hours* turns what could have been simply a very good collection of future standards into a self-contained 48-minute song suite: echoes of Ravel and Debussy in the service of moody American song. (Stanley Kubrick was such a fan of *In the Wee Small Hours* that he hired Riddle to score his film of Nabokov's *Lolita*.) The emphasis is on overall texture (glancingly light, but anchored in deep pulls and purrs of bass) rather than instrumental solos. And quite an odd texture it is too, involving a whole sonic lacework of woodwind, harps, chimes and rustling seven-string guitar. Glacial strings. Beatless languor. The title song begins with a susurration of chimes echoing like church bells in the quiet midnight air. After just a minute and a half, Sinatra falls silent, as if he's broken off teary-eyed to stare at an old photo or refill his glass: for nearly thirty seconds he disappears completely.

In a 1993 essay, 'How We Missed the Saturday Dance', Gore Vidal revealed that his own special Rosebud, a personal mnemonic for loss in general and one particular person lost to the Second World War, was the old standard 'Don't Get around Much Anymore'. There's a clue here to how it is that a lot of supposedly lightweight Easy Listening, far from being merely divertingly kitsch, can contain a whole world of stronger, darker currents. How it often feels, as Apollinaire said of De Quincey, like a 'sweet and chaste and poisoned glass'. On *GB* the horns and strings are sheer Tommy Dorsey phantoms: we might be back in the 1940s, at a ball at the embassy when bombs start to fall. Lyrics that initially seem a bit corny slowly reveal an oblique postwar mood: gratitude tinged with melancholy, love vamped by desperate nostalgia. You've survived – but others haven't. You've survived – but maybe everything seems a bit pale now. Time creeps. Once you bear this in mind, all sorts of innocent-seeming lines take on a different air: 'Now is the hour when we must say goodbye ... I'll miss you far across the sea ... until our hearts have learned to sing again ... roses will die with the summertime ... our roads may be far apart ... when you come home once more ...' A key lyric here is Noël Coward's 'I'll Follow My Secret Heart', and a line which suggests both in-the-closet romance and devious spycraft: 'I'll keep all of my dreams apart ... No matter what price is paid.' (Tinker, Tailor, Soldier, Singer.) This is the feeling you get from so much of Sinatra's singing: it too has a secret heart.

Sinatra combined all the contradictions of postwar America into one immaculate figure. Public confidence and private terrors. Great distances and perplexing intimacy. Single malt and double lives in Miami, Washington, London, Rome. Sinatra is the Cold War torch singer par excellence: unreliable narrator, star witness, mole in his own life. What better song to soundtrack the early 1960s than Sinatra's 'How Little We Know' (1963), which works as a breezy allegory on head-in-the-sand hedonism ('How little we understand ... how ignorant bliss is'), nuclear realpolitik ('that sudden explosion when two tingles intermingle') and early *Mad Men*-style fatalism: 'The world around us shatters / How little it matters.' As JFK-approved envoy for the New Frontier, Sinatra would seem a gift for Western propaganda, a walking billboard for Kapital's 'good life'. But there are many moments in his catalogue

– from *The Manchurian Candidate* (1962) to his strange Cheever-esque musical novella *Watertown* (1970) – when the rosy façade falls away, revealing something far more ambiguous and often pretty gruesome. He was, I think, a man drawn to expressing something light-filled and democratic and orderly, while being all the time acutely aware of the dark chaos within, just below the well-groomed skin.

I've always found Sinatra most seductive, and most disquieting, the softer and more liquidly rapt he gets. The breakthrough work for me, the first Sinatra LP I truly madly fell for, was *Francis Albert Sinatra & Antonio Carlos Jobim* (1967; fallen for circa 1983): one of the quietest albums ever made and – appropriately enough, given its shoreline feel – one of my own Desert Island discs. Ten songs, 28'05", voice never raised above a murmur: utter perfection. A music barely there, like pollen on a summer breeze, the drowsy strings not slathered all over everything, but coming and going like midnight optimism. Sinatra sings lines like 'tall and tan and young and lovely' – all these clicky, tricky consonants like soldiers on guard duty – and yet when you recall his voice it's a soft, uncurling wave.

With bittersweet songs like these, Sinatra never drags you down and empties you out. It's only in the closing years of his career that he brushes against a deeper sadness; there are moments on later albums such as *A Man Alone* (1969), *Watertown* (1970) and *She Shot Me Down* (1981) that do skirt some kind of awful resignation. But if Sinatra can deliver a suicidal lyric without making you feel at all suicidal, it was something he first learned at the feet of his idol among vocalists, Billie Holiday. From Holiday, Sinatra learned a whole new grammar of pause and air: singing aimed not at the big empty auditorium of old but a hypothetical low-lit 3 a.m. room. They were both drawn in song to a certain borderline mood or place: dusk and dawn, beaches and docks, empty streets, lonely horizons. The falling dark, and the becoming light. Songs that map some in-between state close to sleep but wide awake.

Despite all the success and acclaim, there does seem to have been a salt-lick of bitterness about him in the twilight years. My own feeling is that this unhappiness first surfaced in the mid-1960s. There were signs of a breach in his formerly impregnable taste. He recorded songs he really shouldn't have. He married someone he probably shouldn't have. The 1966 Mia Farrow union baffled nearly everyone around Sinatra, even if they didn't say so at the time. We don't know what Dolly Sinatra made of the 21-year-old Farrow's interest in yoga, macrobiotics and ESP. She was almost a cartoonist's caricature of a Hollywood hippie girl, palpably the very opposite of everything Sinatra had ever bared his desiring teeth at in the past. 'Ha!' Ava Gardner quipped, 'I always knew Frank would end up in bed with a little boy.' She also called him a 'scared monster' – but scared of what? Disappearing youth and virility, the bony spectres of mortality? Was Farrow a stick-figure symbol of time(s) both lost and longed for, a fond idea of rejuvenation, of reaching for sweet young flesh like a quirky health-food panacea that might shake him out of a certain unanticipated stasis, when the manoeuvres that had always worked before now just made his Jack hangover feel ten times worse? The melancholy that used to be intermittent now settled in like a permanent crease in his daily fabric. What kind of a world did he look out on, now?

In his half-brilliant Sinatra résumé, *All or Nothing at*

All, Donald Clarke is curtly dismissive of albums such as *A Man Alone* and *Watertown* – works I revere like holy objects. Clarke is great on early and middle period Sinatra but I think he misreads those late works. I can't disagree with him on one thing, though: Sinatra's worst missteps in the second half of his career nearly always involved his covering ill-chosen contemporary pop. It can't have been happenstance that made his mid-1960s attempts at 'happening' rock/pop (including Joni Mitchell's 'Both Sides, Now' – surely a Mia suggestion?) complete flops, whereas more reflective and fatalistic works like *A Man Alone* and *Watertown* sound disarmingly convincing. On *Strangers in the Night* (1966) there is a bizarre version of 'Downtown': the first time I heard it I took it to be a record company mistake, a bum take let through by someone at Reprise who wasn't paying enough attention. 'Downtown!' he choruses, then he makes this strange back-of-the-throat gurgle – eurrrgh – like something sour brought up by that morning's hangover heave. But things are rarely accidental in Sinatra land: that 'eurrrgh' may well be his eyebrows-raised verdict on the song itself, on all those cockamamie songs some suit has obviously suggested he try. There's an equally wince-making version of 'Mrs Robinson' on *My Way* (1969), where his flatline 'woe woe woe, hey hey hey' is the first and last time on record that he sounds utterly disengaged, almost robotic.

Unsuitable material doesn't always produce unmitigated disaster. Given a rich lyric like 'Send in the Clowns', which, strictly speaking, doesn't really suit his voice or persona, Sinatra can still mine the song's emotional core. There's an obvious point here which I think Clarke fudges. He writes of the music as if it were entirely separate from the life, as if the air doesn't feel different at the age of 55 from the way it feels at 21. Well, it does, it feels entirely different. The vividly wistful tone Sinatra manages to infuse his late work with is not quite clown-time happy, but never quite I-give-up depressed. He admits tenderness without admitting defeat. Under it all remains the figure of the only child of immigrant parents, an always gregarious but forever lonely boy. Did it all go back to the over-zealous Dolly and the nebulous Marty? Her love often indistinguishable from censure, his a form of pained absence.

Sinatra kept up a busy itinerary to the very end, singing live at the drop of a hat, trying out new things, doing favours, arranging galas, flying round the world. He got the Presidential Medal of Freedom in 1985 and became something of a Reagan presidency insider. (He became such a White House fixture that he even got his own, slyly perceptive, Secret Service codename: Napoleon.) When he died in 1998, aged 82, it felt oddly anti-climactic. His final recorded works, *Duets* and *Duets II* (1993/94) were, at best, a well-meant misfire, some of the guest performances literally phoned in. But there is one final near-great moment right at the end of *Duets*, when Sinatra waves adieu to his life in song with a deeply affecting 'One for My Baby (and One More for the Road)': 'Could tell you a lot, but you've got to be true to your code.' Certain secrets went safely to the grave.

This year takes in the centenaries of both Frank Sinatra and Billie Holiday: 7 April for Billie, 12 December for Frank. As well as updated biographies and 'officially approved' photo albums, there will doubtless be 'tributes' galore: female vocalists risking ignominy with versions of songs Billie made her own; TV-pop alpha males putting on their shiniest shoes and cheesiest grins and all manner of postmodern ritz to 'do a Sinatra'. And it might take another book-length study to work out why all of this is so fruitless and vainglorious and doomed: why none of it feels in the least bit convincing.

When today's stars try to pull off an imitation of old-style song craft they may get the surface details right, but they completely miss the centre of gravity, or sense of connective purpose. They can't locate Sinatra's lightness of touch, or his deep seriousness. They can't 'do' Sinatra because the latter didn't 'do' easy, imitable exaggerations. His tone was toned right down; his slow-burn intensity came from somewhere deep inside. Even in his own era, when most MOR acts would usually opt to open out a song, inflate the hook, make everything big and brassy, Sinatra would take the mood down a notch, hypnotizing the song's back brain with hints of smoke, perfume, shoreline air. Sinatra held the melody like a Fabergé egg he was turning about in his palm, assessing it from every angle, seeing how light dipped or flared in different positions, exploring the weave of word and melody.

None of this can be applied like spray tan. It's probably not something that can even be 'learned' any longer. Instead, our TV ironists ape the outermost skin: the 'iconic' package of Sinatra's ring-a-ding profile and razor-blade hat brim and cheesy 'Hey now!' persona. Starting in the late 1960s, Sinatra did occasionally cede flashes of send-up fun with his own persona; but fundamentally, he may be the last big mainstream entertainer to perform without carefully applied quotation marks. We are probably not far off a time when he will seem, to many young pop consumers, as singularly odd and inconceivable a figure as a long-ago scrivener or apothecary.

During the final ebb-tide years Sinatra would close all his concerts with a little speech in which he offered the audience his own special seigneurial benediction: the same kind of luck he'd had, peace of mind, an enduring song of love. 'And may the last voice you hear be mine...' From anyone else it might seem a bit hokey and presumptuous, but from Sinatra it felt like the punchline to a fondly shared and long-cherished gag. He was speaking to everyone in the audience who'd grown up with that voice and grown old with that face, and forgiven their owner's many trespasses. He'd been their fall guy and idol, political bellwether and stand-in Las Vegas libertine. They'd played his records on first dates and then later at wakes for army buddies and others gone too soon. No one else's voice seemed to play just so on so many different occasions. 'In the roaring traffic's boom, in the silence of my lonely room...'

Perhaps Sinatra's voice will increasingly come to seem like one of the last things nearly everyone could agree on, and rough out some kind of aesthetic consensus around, in the final flicker of modernity's embers. It's doubtful any singer will ever again possess that kind of sway. Who could reign as monarch of so much territory, and certainty, ever again? Maybe he is our last voice, at that.

THE FAST BIRTH AND SLOW OEDIPAL
DEATH OF ELVIS AARON PRESLEY

In the spring of 1965, on the road between Memphis and
Hollywood, desert plains all around, his bloodstream
torqued by a tinnital static of prescription ups and
downs, Elvis Presley finally broke down. He poured
out his troubles to Larry Geller, celebrity hair stylist
and, lately, something of a spirit guide for Elvis. Geller
had given him a mind-expanding reading list of what
we would now recognize as New Age self-help books.
Elvis had read them all, performed all the meditations,
but didn't feel the light, not in mind, body or soul. The
fire refused to descend; his spiritual air remained a vac-
uum. Now, on the plush customized tour bus, Geller
was thrown by how desperate Elvis seemed. Flailing,
he fished out a Zen koan: 'If you want tea, first empty
your cup.' (Tea? Empty cups? This was not the language
Elvis spoke. His cup would require several lifetimes'
scouring.)

Later that afternoon, at a site near the Grand Canyon,
everything tilted on its axis. Elvis grabbed Geller's arm
and pointed out of the bus at some distant clouds, shout-
ing: 'Look! There's Joseph Stalin in the clouds! What is
he doing up there?' He had the bus stop, and ran into the
desert. 'Oh my God, Larry, follow me!' Elvis was bab-
bling, tears running down his face. He grabbed Geller,
hugged him and said: 'You're right: you told me the
truth. God is love.' The sky had not turned the colour
of cherry yoghurt, he didn't hear night dogs howling at
the sunlight, or the screech of messenger crows. Now
that it had finally arrived, his vision was sharp and
clear, trailing a flavour more of banishment than revelation – banishment and shame. Stalin, he thought,

was a message about the Evil Elvis inside, his goatish ego. Stalin's face dissolved into a knife-point pain in his heart, became a slow-motion explosion, became the face of Christ. This was clearly a defining moment: today and tomorrow would be as different as land and sky.

That evening, safe in his Bel Air rental (a Frank Lloyd Wright designed house previously owned by the Shah of Iran), he said to Geller: 'I don't want to perform any more. I want to leave the world. Find me a monastery. I want to become a monk.' But his ascetic mood soon passed (as every Elvis mood passed, each brief and delicious horripilation), and the marker of this grand spiritual event became an order he put in to his personal jeweller for two hundred wrist watches that flashed both cross of Jesus and star of David. Such personal touches were far more Elvis than any of the books that had been recommended to him. Soon life would again be games with lascivious starlets and golden guns and awesome dune buggies. Soon he would be home again and primed for every day's hijinks; soon it would be night again and every night's endless waking sleep.

Elvis Aaron Presley was born on 8 January 1935 at around 4.30 in the morning, at home in East Tupelo. His older twin, Jesse Garon, was stillborn. (There was ugly gossip later that the doctor, William Robert Hunt, might have had a drink; that he might have saved Jesse if he hadn't been so preoccupied with the surprise appearance of a second child. But the Presleys were satisfied with his work and Dr Hunt received his standard $15 payment from the county.) In many communities the arrival of twins was regarded as a queasy, unreadable omen. What to make of this mixed benison of one dead and one surviving lamb? Elvis was born into a puzzle, a world marked by loss from the start. From his first breath, life would always be a matter of missing echoes – conversations that could only be imagined, a partnership annulled before it could even begin – but for his deeply religious mother there was never any doubt: he was chosen, blessed, her own golden king.

All through the pregnancy, Gladys Presley had attended her local Baptist church, the Tabernacle of the Assembly of God. This was a Pentecostal faith in which the happy ordeal of being born again was called the 'burning love'; speaking in tongues was considered a gift – variously known as 'the barks', 'the jerks' or 'the Holy laugh' – and parishioners were encouraged to rise and speak at any time, allowing God's voice to pour out from within. Gladys was blessed with this ability, called 'the comin' through'. And that starry forcefield Elvis later stumbled into, where his raucous and playful spirit brought the whole world to his blue-shod feet – wasn't that too a form of 'comin' through'? Gladys would live to see her boy-king ascend to heaven (or its earthly equivalent, the *Ed Sullivan Show*) but her own humbled body gave up the ghost in August 1958. In a family portrait taken two months earlier she looks absent, distracted. Her eyes seem to float out beyond the frame, as if she has already sighted the star-shape of death, felt some sharp feather of pain worse even than losing a child. 'She's my best girlfriend,' Elvis sobbed on the white steps of Graceland when she was gone: 'She's all we lived for.'

Before she met Elvis's father, she was Gladys Love Smith. Her mother was Octavia Luvenia Mansell, her great-grandmother was a Cherokee, Morning White Dove. These were stoical and wilful women; whereas the Presley men were not what you'd call an unmixed blessing. Elvis's great-grandfather, Dunnan Presley Jr, was a two-time Civil War deserter. When he had to fill out a form for a government pension, he wrote: 'I depend upon myself and do the best I can, which is bad.' As Peter Whitmer puts it in *The Inner Elvis* (1996), 'there was a history to the emptiness that flawed Vernon's character and created the subsequent psychological hole in Elvis's personality. Both the lack of and the need for a father figure seemed to be a Presley family tradition.' Vernon Presley struck his neighbours as amiable enough, but not all there: a man of hollow promises, fundamentally unreliable. Sometimes he seemed to be little more than a lazy impersonator of his own cherished self-image – airy, cunning, one of life's happy drifters. He ended up in the penitentiary, following a poor attempt at forgery. If he'd only been a tiny bit smarter, he might have made one hell of a con artist.

This year's Elvis anniversary is one of the happier ones. It's sixty years since the summer night in a small Memphis studio when the 19-year-old Elvis set his flag in the pop-cultural soil with two convulsively unselfconscious performances: 'That's Alright' and its eventual b-side, 'Blue Moon of Kentucky'. Helped along by the wired know-how of studio owner Sam Phillips, Elvis and two rockabilly cats he'd only just met made a devilishly catchy new sound out of country dash and bluesy holler and after-hours leer. The name of the studio was Sun: flash, heat, escaping light. Ra worship in this other Memphis. Teenage culture's own A-bomb, with so much fallout to come.

It's debatable whether those first recordings can now contain all the weight they've been made to carry. What is there is unmistakeable: Elvis's laughing-gas exuberance and obvious delight at his own just accepted dare; Scotty Moore's rattlesnake guitar; Bill Black's rail-jumping bass. You can find the music itself a bit thin, jerky, underwhelming, and still see why it ignited all the brush fires up ahead. (In sonic terms, Moore and Phillips were probably far more influential than Elvis. Phillips's use of echo on those early sides is startling – in his mid-1950s pomp he got a sound it would take the Rolling Stones until 1972's *Exile on Main Street* to secure. And Keith Richards says he still can't work out some of Moore's blistering riffs and runs.) Listening to these itchy little songs in your front room, sixty years on, you miss the most vital spark in the detonation: Elvis's own vivid, mercurial presence. His heat and his motion. His grin and his shimmy. His robes and his finery.

One side of the young Elvis was a faultlessly polite, radiantly ordinary boy next door. But he was also drawn to outrageous clothes, pimpish overload, endless resculpting of his princely hair. His everyday clothes look neither work-appropriate, nor what was then officially classy. The way he looked says 'underclass and proud of it', but also frames an utterly personal dream of light and colour: arcs of pink and black, sunrise yellow and winter frost. Hacksaw sharp and baked-peach luscious. Elvis may not have been much of an actor, but he was surely made to be looked at. Boys wanted to move like him, girls wanted to unwrap him like an expensive Easter chocolate. Odd, glancing hints of femininity in his make-up (and, indeed, his make-up) distinguished him from contemporary rockabilly dudes like Jerry Lee Lewis, Johnny Cash and Carl Perkins. He found an obvious joy in the staged act of seduction: the body does brazen, while the face remains convincingly bashful.

Pamela Clarke Keogh's *Elvis: The Man. The Life. The Legend* (2004) is mostly what you'd expect from an official biography ('written with the assistance of Elvis Presley Enterprises'): a jaunty soft-pedal, wisps of lonely cloud against lovely Hawaiian skies rather than bruises and darkness. But Keogh has a subtly wary eye and slips in some shrewdly bittersweet undertones: 'Beneath his extraordinary politeness he has the docility of a house servant.' The traditional view is that the alchemy in Elvis's crucible was black carnality sieved through white restraint. But what if it was the other way round, or no simple way round at all, and far odder? Every Elvis biography makes it clear that even initial enemies were won over by the boy's good manners. But it's hard not to hear in Keogh's 'house servant' the echo of a far less neutral phrase: 'house nigger'. Maybe what mainstream America embraced and accepted in Elvis was a magic switcheroo of black politeness and white carnality. For some folks back then, 'cracker' was as offensive a term as 'nigger', and 'hillbilly' was as much a musicological label as 'negro' or 'race'. When Southern boy Elvis first went north to do some fancy New York TV, the usually quite hep Steve Allen miscalculated badly and showcased him in a dreary, patronizing skit in which Elvis has to deliver his song to an actual slobbery hound dog. You can feel the Northern condescension and snobbery thick like molasses in the studio air. For his second TV appearance on *Ed Sullivan*, Elvis was treated like some kind of Tennessee-bred Ebola virus in peg-leg pants. The line this time was drawn between the north and south of his own spasmodic body, a prophylactic Mason-Dixon line somewhere around the belt loops.

The old saw about Elvis 'ripping off' black music is a bit of a non-starter. If he forged anything new from old stock, it was hard-bopping country music that was used

103

as a baseline. Presley's early Sun-side rhythms are all train-whistle country and sickle-moon bluegrass. The black rhythm and blues originals of songs like 'Hound Dog' and 'Mystery Train' are taken far more slowly – they have an undulant, rough-tongued chug. Elvis's 'Hound Dog' is pure kids' cartoon alongside Big Mama Thornton's hot-breathed growl. Elvis's musical lift-off was never a simple black and white equation; it was more like a backroom radio left on between stations to pick up a tingly mix of all the different sounds in the air that month. Back then, a lot of country music was pretty hip and driven and freaky. (It also had a legion of strong front women, just like Gladys Presley.) The echoes Elvis carried into his own jump-up song were mainly of white artists like Jimmie Rodgers and Gene Autry. Even Elvis's urbane hero Dean Martin made goo-goo eyes at the country market: 'Night Train to Memphis' from 1951 lays his languid, soothing croon over a curvy seesaw beat, and seems to predict quite a bit of the Elvis aesthetic to come. Bill Haley – Presley's immediate rival for rock and roll trailblazer – started out as Bill Haley and the Four Aces of Western Swing, before he saw where the real pension dollars were. Hank Williams had already taken a lot of the corn out of country and amped up the backbeat. Williams's style was unashamedly backwoods, though, his son-of-a-gun accent upfront (when he sings 'I don't care if tomorrow never comes' the 'care' comes out as a sharply elongated hiccup: 'keeeey-air'); he would always have been too feral-seeming and unstable to qualify for real mainstream crossover, even if he hadn't died young.

Elvis's real wildcard was his face: he had the kind of protean good looks amenable to wildly differing interpretations and lusts. He was an irresistible blank that different audience members could project their own private fantasies onto. If you look through early photos of Elvis you can't help but notice a blurry, shapeshifter effect. He's like certain shamans, who according to legend display complete fluidity of gender: male woman, female man. In one photo Elvis looks sordid and leering; in another, pure choirboy. From snap to snap you pick up all kinds of unlikely lineaments: native American, Mexican, butch 1980s lesbian. The effect is hard to pin down – polymorphous instability? In the end, why deny it, he's just plain gorgeous. He's rough trade for everyone, a true American democracy. It's hardly surprising that one of the first things Presley's new manager, Colonel Tom Parker, did was to get him a big Hollywood contract. He was made to be photographed.

Although he has been execrated by successive generations of Elvis fans, there is a good case for seeing Parker as just as much of a visionary as Sam Phillips. Whatever his flaws and blind spots, Parker was not a stupid man. He had been taught human psychology on the carnival midway and could read people (and contracts) in a flash. From the very first he seems to have seen through to the essence of the young raw Elvis. He sensed a soul wide open – a kid who was monstrously acquisitive, but also fundamentally passive, looking to be counselled and led. In his own wholly pragmatic way, Parker foresaw several future directions that showbiz would take. He saw how Elvis, the real Elvis, with all his moods and problems, could be left to sit at home and do whatever he did, while the spangly, malleable Elvis image could be sent out into the world to work. Parker never used words like 'demographic' or 'synergy', but he had an intuitive understanding of markets and how to exploit them. In the early teen-scream era he had

I HATE ELVIS badges run up to sell to the anti-Presley brigade. Similarly, Parker's reported reaction when Presley died – 'this changes nothing' – cuts to the heart of a certain unsentimental grasp of things. Wasn't it the truth? Hasn't the arc of the subsequent posthumous career only proved it so? Ghost Elvis can take on far more forms than real-life sweaty, disaffected Elvis ever could, and can be in many more places at once: he's far more haunting dead than alive.

By the end of the 1960s, Presley's looks were thickening and his Hollywood servitude was finally played out. His idea of a good time now was to be drug-coddled, bed-bound, lecturing a circle of paid friends on some latest fixation. Finding the Third Eye. Realizing the Inner God. Psychic sex. (He could, it seems, bore for Buddha.) And then there were the other obsessions. In three days in 1970 he bought $20,000 worth of guns in one store alone. His favourite people to hang out with by this point were cops, especially drug cops. His favourite movie to watch and memorize and watch again was *Patton: Lust for Glory*. Music didn't really compete much any more, but when he did find a song he liked he played it to death. At the height of this drugged-up, locked-down, gun-limned period he found one song that took his breath away, and stuck it on auto-repeat for whole frazzled nights at a time. It was the British light entertainer Roger Whittaker's 'The Last Farewell'.

Presley may genuinely not have realized how far gone into addiction he was, because unlike most addicts he never had to go without. With his very own circle of tame doctors (the kind Burroughs would call 'real writing croakers') he never had any kind of crisis with supply and demand. He demanded, they supplied.

Elvis's biggest drug problem was that he had no problem getting drugs. Foremost among his legal drug suppliers was the infamous Dr Nick, George C. Nichopoulos. For one ten-day tour in 1977, Nichopoulos secured 682 different pills and tablets for Elvis, plus the dauntingly strong narcotic Dilaudid in liquid form. It was later established in court that in the seven months before Presley's death the good doctor had prescribed 8,805 pills, tablets, vials and injectables. Elvis also had regular supplies coming in from other star-struck doctors. One night, Nichopoulos accompanied Elvis to the dentist; when the dentist briefly left the room, even Dr Nick could hardly believe his eyes as Elvis began to scrabble around the surgery in a desperate search for codeine.

Presley's drug reliance initially took hold during his army posting to Germany in the late 1950s – the period when true-blue fans claim the real bad-boy Elvis was effectively neutered. While off base in Bad Nauheim – it was in some sense appropriate that it should have been an old spa town – he was introduced to prescription amphetamine and became an avid proselytizer. When the 14-year-old Priscilla first fetched up in Elvis's boudoir and was having trouble adjusting to his night-for-day timetable, out came the little Sunkist-coloured vials. She blanched, Elvis soothed. If it was in the *Physicians' Desk Reference* it was not a 'drug' drug. If he thought it was a 'drug' drug he'd have nothing to do with it! (Maybe this made more sense at a time when avuncular, white-coated surgeons routinely advertised cigarettes.) The trouble with running your metabolism on amphetamine rails is the eventual nerve-jangled crash. And what better way to offset the hyperintense zig of speed than with the zzzzaaaaag of some new soporific? Without even noticing, you've already slipped into a way of dealing with life's quandaries that is entirely chemical in its logic.

A day in the life: pure liquid cocaine soaked into cotton balls and stuffed up his nose for breakfast; a tutti-frutti of eviscerating biphetamines to get the day off to a smart jog; a whole undulant funhouse spin of downs, any downs at all, for tea. And yet, and yet ... Presley's excess never feels particularly Dionysian; it seems far more a matter of itinerary and control. Sex and drugs were never binged things, but run always according to his pernickety little schedules. In the 2005 photo history *Elvis by the Presleys*, there are two books embossed with his special golden name-stamp: a slim black *New Testament Prayer Key* and his colossal, multi-coloured *Physicians' Desk Reference*. (The latter was his bible, next to the Bible.) Life became more and more a closed-off space, Graceland a cathedral dedicated to endless self-reflection. He was his own icon, long before he became ours.

All this livid Late Elvis stuff, all the tales of shot-out TV sets and shot-up tranqs, would eventually return him to a dark kind of semi-hipness. Punk, far from banishing Presley, brought him back to life as a kind of negative totem. He epitomised Bad America. He epitomised Decadent Rock. He epitomized how sick and alienated mainstream society really was behind closed doors. With its veneer of sneer, punk was really the last burst of teenage sincerity, a cry of real confusion, hurt and rage; far from being a denial of venerable rock history, it was the last stop on the line. Punk and Elvis may not have got into bed together, but there was definitely some Oedipal tension in the mucosal late 1970s air.

Early in *Elvis Has Left the Building* Dylan Jones, the editor of GQ, brushes against some of the paradoxes of

Elvis in the age of punk. But it never goes much further than that. We get nearly as much of the author's own biography as Presley's: small-town rock obsessive, punk convert, London squatter, art college blade. How much light does this shine on Elvis? Not a lot. Plus, it's pretty much a straight replay of a nearly identical chapter in Jones's 2005 book *iPod, Therefore I Am*. The new title reads a lot like some flashy magazine's Elvis special: a bit of memoir, a bit of fashion, a bit of a superficial round-up of what was going on in 1977 ('as you drove to the movie theatre you were probably listening to Fleetwood Mac's *Rumours*'); and, of course, a big long 'must-have' list to end on. (Lists! Where would modern sort-of-journalism be without them?) Strangely, in the iPod memoir, where Jones tallies up every pop song he has ever liked or even half-listened to, Elvis is notable by his absence. Among the more than four thousand vital iPod transfers, how many are by Elvis? Not one. And now Jones gives us yet another list, of ... the fifty greatest Elvis tracks.

The iPod book doesn't pretend to be anything other than what it is: you can skim through it in half an afternoon, argue the toss, make your own alternative lists. *Elvis Has Left the Building* is more problematically stranded between glib pose-striking and serious reflection. There are all manner of dubious truisms: 'Everyone over a certain age can remember exactly where they were when they found out that Elvis was dead.' Can they really? I asked a bunch of friends roughly my own (and Jones's) age and not one had a clue where they were when Elvis died. I certainly don't. Maybe we were all having too much teenage fun, or trauma, to notice. By 1977, his final year on earth, Elvis was no longer a particularly big deal for most people. You occasionally saw one of his rictus-faced Hollywood vehicles on tea-time TV and shivered and thought no more about it. 'The amazing story of Elvis, punk and how the star who changed everything lives on,' Jones's cover shouts. But how does this ghostly 'living on' work, exactly? Why do we assent so greedily to the current insane overload of 'iconic' this-and-that and endless minor anniversaries? What is behind this pathological collective nostalgia? Unfortunately (but perhaps not surprisingly, given his day job) Jones doesn't really pry into any of this. How *does* Elvis live on? How exactly does it work for this guy whose terribly inconsistent back catalogue is rarely heard any more; whose completely time-locked films (with the consistency of week-old candyfloss) are never seen; and whose pretty rank persona – sexist, reactionary, NRA-supporting, Nixon-voting – is not what you'd call a hot selling point for any potential new young fans. Why isn't he, as Paddy McAloon so memorably put it, 'as obsolete as warships in the Baltic'? Jones briefly engages with the workings of the whole 'icon' industry in his penultimate chapter on Graceland, but he's too much a happy gatekeeper of the very same world to 'wear his game face' (his own phrase) for this investigation.

I also can't forgive Jones for leaving my own all-time favourite track off a 'best of Elvis' list: his soft, spooky, haunting version of 'Blue Moon'. I have to admit, I would struggle to put together such a list: I always thought Elvis worked far better in occasional jukebox bursts than extended play. It was only recently that I came across a collection I could listen to from start to finish: *Elvis at Stax* (2013) assembles tracks from various mid-1970s sessions at the label's Memphis studios. Elvis sounds relaxed with his material and gives the songs genuine, mood-sensitive readings, rather than just one more hip-roll run through. He sounds like what he is: a man in looming middle age, no longer sure which way is up. He's lived a bit, done some bad bad things, survived the odd crisis. He's been up in the righteous sky and down in the mole-claw dirt. Now when he ghosts through a bluesy plaint it sounds thoroughly convincing. Even some brief bursts of between-song banter are revealing. Elvis hums to himself, warming up his voice. He starts out in light gospel mode ('Further along...'), then branches off into a different song or a different line of thought: 'Wasted years...' He repeats the phrase and draws the 'wasted' out like a great long fragile fan: 'Oh, how foolish...' In a song called 'Help Me', he sounds as if he's finally crawled to a Narcotics Anonymous meeting: 'With a humble heart, on bended knees, I'm begging you please: help me!'

Singers like Isaac Hayes (a Stax act, as it happens) had already shown that MOR balladry could be a many-splendoured trip, and with the best songs in the Stax selection we finally get to hear both sides of Elvis: good twin, bad twin; the creepy and threatening Elvis as well as the more familiar croony sentimentalist. Billy Goldenberg, the musical director of Presley's 1968 'comeback' TV special, saw just such buried qualities in Elvis, and later spelled it out for Presley's biographer Jerry Hopkins: 'There's a cruelty involved, there's a meanness, there's a basic sadistic quality about what he does. He's excited by certain kinds of violent things.'

The smiley glad-handing Elvis always exhibited in public when meeting people for the first time had its roots in a richly ambiguous tradition of Southern 'good manners', a whole codified arrangement – whatever the colour of user and recipient – in grey. I had high hopes that Joel Williamson's *Elvis Presley: A Southern Life* might

take Presley's background seriously – even over-se-
riously. Academic treatments of pop culture can be
hard-going over the course of a whole bulky text, but if
they throw out a few unusual perspectives, loopy con-
ceptual reframings, then all to the good. (The real place
to look for this right now is – I'm not kidding – the ever
expanding area of Elvis impersonator studies: life imitating Don DeLillo.) Sadly, *A Southern Life* is not really
an academic/theoretical study at all, just one more solid
biography. It's not a bad book by any means, but it wasn't
crying out to be written after Peter Guralnick's defini-
tive two-volume *Life*.[3] In his preface, Williamson ticks off
several interesting areas (sex, race, notions of 'Southern
womanhood') but then doesn't go anywhere with them.
He throws out a few obligatory references to William
Faulkner and Tennessee Williams, but without further
elucidation this comes across as lazy, almost random.
Why not Harry Crews? Why not Flannery O'Connor?
Why not (note the initials) Edgar Allan Poe? Why not
the Beverley Hillbillies? Elvis, Tennessee Williams,
Faulkner: can you think of three less similar people?
Even the fact of their Southern birth doesn't really
haunt their work in any consonant manner. Faulkner
and Williams both needed isolation to do their work.
With Elvis, after he hit it big you wonder if he was ever

3   *The Inner Elvis: A Psychological Biography of Elvis Aaron Presley*,
    by Peter Whitmer (1996), a book I found in a local charity shop,
    turned out to be far better on the South and Elvis's fateful family
    psychology. Whitmer's shrink-ish lingo teeters on the edge of
    overwrought ('Death rehearsal... psychological bleeding... mood
    congruent delusion') and some of his speculation about Elvis
    as 'twinless twin' seems a bit over-schematic; but at its best the
    writing has a livid, startled plausibility. He does Elvis and his
    family/culture the due compliment of taking them altogether
    seriously.

again, even for one minute, alone. Meanwhile, for all the good-time buddies, the pliant showgirls, the downpour of narcotics, you feel his loneliness just got deeper and sharper and more claustrophobic; that it became almost a tangible, breathing thing, a companion for the early hours when all the day's games and monologues were finally through. A replacement twin.

Elvis died on 16 August 1977, aged 42. He was over-weight, over-medicated and had been poring over a paperback called *The Scientific Search for the Face of Jesus*. When success first hit in 1956 he was 21, and had seen nothing of the world outside Tupelo and Memphis. That kind of outsize success for this kind of backwoods child was a wholly new phenomenon, and anyone might have struggled with the psychological backwash. Presley seems to have gone into a form of spooked retreat al-most immediately. He erected a shell of bland politesse and jokey normality, hid in plain sight. Yes sir, he said to all the reporters. No ma'am, to all the society ladies and concerned mothers of America. Yes sir, no ma'am – to Colonel Tom, to RCA, to Hollywood, to Priscilla Beaulieu's parents, to the United States Army. A yes and a no that measured a whole wild world of material change, but not, perhaps, very much disruption of his own fundamentally passive nature. A huge wash of suc-cess, out on all the stages of the world. Inside, though, his world contracted to the size of a luxurious but air-less crypt, filled with fossilized dreams, live corpses, the chatter of ghosts.

Elvis remains the unbeatable blueprint for rock and roll lift-off: a combination of heroic self-invention and giving the world something it only just realized it had to have. But he also remains the template for how to deal badly with all the accompanying fame and success. Each discrete and blithely choreographed step: the dubious manager; the thoroughly personalized but oddly impersonal mansion; the slow crumbling turn inward; the scattering of original friends; the self-embalming drug fall; the painful evaporation of work and sociability. Elvis really did do everything first – even the not doing, even the not being.

HALF IN LOVE WITH BLIND JOE DEATH:
GUITAR VIRTUOSO JOHN FAHEY'S
AMERICAN ODYSSEY

The acoustic guitarist John Fahey was one of those musicians who exist just below the hosanna of popular acclaim: awkward savants who may not shift a colossal number of 'units' but have a profound effect on those who fall under their spell. Fahey first came to public attention in the mid-1960s, when he put out records on his own Takoma label. (The independent musician-trader is no recent invention.) He was then rediscovered in the 1970s by people like me, searching for nuggets of useful treasure in the pre-punk margins; then found again in the 1990s, by assorted post-Nirvana refugees in need of restorative light after the death-howl of grunge. Within certain musical scenes, Fahey's influence is provably indispensable.

When I was a callow young learner-strummer, I couldn't for the life of me work out how down-home pickers like Fahey did what they did: it sounded at once so elegantly simple and yet musicologically baffling and opaque. (Before computer downloads and the easy-to-parse 'tablature' method of musical transcription, the only way to figure out this stuff was some unlikely meeting with a clued-in elder, who might pass on the secrets of the six-string sodality.) So much early rock guitar focused on the flashy runs made by a player's pyro-athletic left hand: how fast and grandiloquently fussy (as well as shatteringly loud) things could be made to sound. Fahey emerged from – and merged with – a wholly different tradition. In the technique termed 'fingerpicking', perfected by the Delta blues guitarists of the 1920s and 1930s, emphasis switches to the right hand: your thumb hammers out a beat on the three strings lowest in tone (nearest your chin: E-A-D) while the other four fingers pick out melodic runs on the three strings highest in tone (nearest your knee: G-B-E). The unwearying thumb does the work of an entire rhythm section, while the other fingers pick out more unpredictable slides and sorties. Every string has a potential tale: jagged or leafy, rueful or resilient. For first-time listeners, it may sound like two guitarists playing at once in judicious harmony, a modest instrument made glancingly symphonic.

For me, this particular door creaked open via a helpfully cheap 1970s compilation – *The Contemporary Guitar Sampler, Volume 1* – which I recently relocated in a seedy charity-shop pile. Most of the featured players (Bert Jansch and John Renbourn, among others) were plucked from a still-healthy British folk scene. Fahey sounded different: his near-parched mood music felt less fussy, more straightforward, yet also somehow eerie and hard to place.

Fahey was one of the young white American kids who discovered folk and blues music in the early 1960s and took their epiphany off in two markedly different directions. One, the slightly larger group, became the rather po-faced purists of the hugely popular folk revival (Fahey had big problems with both the music and politics of this group). The other, blown away by the songs assembled on the likes of Harry Smith's *Anthology of American Folk Music*, tried to fashion appropriately idiomatic forms of their own in which to recast the old, uncanny spell. Groups like the Grateful Dead, which ended up broadcasting psychedelic apocalypse through huge speaker cabinets, had their roots in a world of beardy bluegrass obsessives and coffeehouse picking circles.

When Fahey started collecting old 78 RPM records, his primary musical fetish was bluegrass, too – a music that could come across as both bruisingly up-tempo and hauntingly tender. The music of Bill Monroe, Roscoe Holcomb, and the Carter Family would rattle along like an out-of-control freight train; in more reflective moments, it let loose what folklorist John Cohen called its distinctive 'high lonesome sound'. Run on an odd, loping shuffle, bluegrass can ambush unwary listeners with its askew and spacious harmonies. The impression it leaves can be unsettling: an apparently humble music of homestead and family that also feels like it's trying to pick up enough steam to outrun its own shadow. As a committed bluegrass fan, Fahey was initially quite sniffy, even condescending, about blues music: getting inside the stop-go technique of bluegrass was one thing, but the anguished intensity of the blues was something else again, a Faustian zone that the young Fahey wasn't ready to access. But this teenage churchgoer and future philosophy student had a few shadows in his own basement. Hidden at the heart of the blues – and Fahey's own small-town worldview – was a good deal of white-hot anger.

One day, a fellow music obsessive put on 'Praise God I'm Satisfied', a scratchy old 78 by Blind Willie Johnson, and Fahey's world shifted on its axis. He felt (in his own words) 'nauseated', and then burst into floods of tears. In the morning, he was one person; by the end of the day, 'it was the start of the rest of my life'. He later called it a 'hysterical conversion experience', and it determined both his subsequent musical career and dependably contrarian worldview. He became consumed by blues guitar and began tracking down some of its forgotten early innovators. He wrote a scholarly book on the backwoods ecstatic Charley Patton. Fahey's empathy for the raw emotional potency of such musicians also fed his distaste for the folk revivalism then current; he really despised these prim, better-world folkies, though he may have seen something in their smugly elitist attitude that he recognized from his own pre-conversion outlook.

Fahey merged the dark voodoo of the Delta blues with his own off-kilter sense of American self, nature, and space. His earliest home recordings show a young musician dedicated, occasionally nimble, but still very much a fond copyist. But by 1965 and his watershed LP, *The Transfiguration of Blind Joe Death*, we hear a different proposition altogether. His confidence on the guitar is now sharp and beguiling: he transforms even the hokey standard 'A Bicycle Built for Two' into a small jewel of measured compression. Alongside this musical progress, Fahey was piecing together a kind of patchwork personal mythology, composed of a range of personal totems: nature lore (with an abiding fondness for turtles); plantation antiquarianism; and names of ex-girlfriends and apocryphal old bluesmen. This half-jokey imitation of mythic gravitas proved timely and attractive for a young audience beginning to lace flowers in its hair and trade in the conventional suburban pieties for 'Underground Comix' and Carlos Castaneda. A slightly queasy state of affairs obtained, where Fahey's collections of sober and unvarnished folk music came complete with mind-boggling psychedelic sleeve notes, including the flowery text on the back of a 1969 British reissue that signs off with, 'Love and Pies, SUPERSCRIBE'.

Born in 1939, Fahey had, by most accounts (except, much later, a questionably revisionist one of his own), a fairly regular upbringing. His childhood, spent in the leafy Washington, DC, suburb of Takoma Park, Maryland, was neither wildly happy nor soul-crushingly awful. In a 2014 biography, *Dance of Death: The Life of John Fahey, American Guitarist*, writer Steve Lowenthal describes postwar Takoma Park as a place that 'straddled both sides of the racial and cultural divide, with some areas increasingly liberal and others that hung close to old Southern ideologies'. (Fahey would later record an oddly dignified and affecting 'Old Southern Medley'.) Contemporaries may have found the teenage Fahey too intense, but he remained an enthusiastic participant in a number of more or less 'square' social scenes. Fahey wasn't some wild and gnarly beatnik, damning bourgeois 'Amerikkka', but neither was he playing things entirely straight; if he had no intention of settling down into the quiescent Cheeverville of his parents' generation, neither did he trust the daffy new truisms of an emergent counterculture.

Fahey didn't make many new friends with his scything dismissal of the folk revival. He distrusted the way that folkies regarded music as a carrier for the correct political messages of the moment. As Lowenthal puts it: 'To him, the student idealists had naïve worldviews and dreamed of unrealistic political utopias', whereas Fahey 'attempted to channel darkness and dread through his music'. For Woody Guthrie and Pete Seeger devotees, the ideological message came first, with musical tone or trickery a distant second. As Fahey saw it, the dizzyingly strange source music they borrowed from and then built their careers on emerged as little more than a scrubbed-up ventriloquist's doll, all the coarse grain

119

and troubling metaphysic of its original voices jetti-soned. He also detected high condescension and low reverse racism in how the folk-revival people preferred their old blues guys barefoot and wearing dungarees – even if they now usually dressed in sharp suits and often preferred to play amplified, electric urban blues.

Frankfurt School philosopher Theodor Adorno, who some might expect to hold the contrary position, thought that 'politically sound' pop music may have been the worst pop music of all: 'I believe, in fact, that attempts to bring political protest together with popular music – that is, with entertainment music – are doomed from the start.' In the strummy protest music of the early 1960s, the stripping away of all sonic fripperies left a meagre aesthetic: just the brave truth teller and his rough, purposeful guitar in the good, honest, bracing open air. Fahey's music, by comparison, looked back to older examples of the pastoral uncanny in American culture, as hinted at in the titles of some of his singular new compositions: 'The Downfall of the Adelphi Rolling Grist Mill'; 'View (East from the Top of the Riggs Road / B&O Trestle)'; 'The Singing Bridge of Memphis, Tennessee'.

Fahey set about mixing up an inimitable sonic gum-bo of the various musics he personally loved: Charles Ives and Edgard Varèse, blues anguish and Indian raga, Appalachian picking. He went from playing a spirited but limited facsimile of American blues to ever strang-er forms of musical synthesis. He aspired to a kind of semi-acoustic *musique concrète*, which blossomed on al-bums like *The Yellow Princess* (1968) and *Fare Forward Voyagers* (1973). This stylistic turn proved a perfect soundtrack for the moment – plainly and brooding-ly American but also quite trippy at the edges – and soon Fahey could barely keep up with public demand. Between 1967 and 1969, he released five full-length albums, as well as reissuing all his earlier LPs in spiffy new packaging. A 1968 Christmas album even crossed over into the burgeoning Christian market; and, by the early 1970s, Fahey was fielding the seductive propositions of numerous big labels. In 1973, he signed with the Warner Brothers subsidiary Reprise.

Fahey's experimental turn attracted the uncritical attention of an acid-rock audience he felt distinctly uncomfortable with, especially considering his distaste for middle-class 'phonies'. Lowenthal offers his own account of an infamous meeting between Fahey and the filmmaker Michelangelo Antonioni, who wanted some appropriately 'happening' music for his awful (but absolutely on trend, as we now say) 1970 film *Zabriskie Point*. That there are at least three versions of what really transpired between the flinty American guitarist and the brooding Italian director – one account has them coming to blows – doesn't lessen the episode's tragicomic charge.

Fahey was no one's idea of a great businessman, but he was canny enough, at least initially, to engage the right kind of people to work behind the scenes for his small Takoma label, which he started in the late 1950s: people who might take care of all the more practical business he himself disdained. Fahey had a tendency to present himself as far less worldly and pragmatic than he was. He had a keen eye for new talent, and Takoma had a huge success with the brilliant young guitarist Leo Kottke. Fahey's instincts were consistently ahead of the times: in the 1990s, he formed his second label, Revenant Records, which went on to clock up four Grammy awards for its faultlessly researched archive collections.

Before then, however, things had taken a darker turn. Fahey's sale of Takoma in 1981 marked the beginning of a personal and professional decline. At some point in the 1980s, he contracted Epstein-Barr virus (aka chronic fatigue syndrome), exacerbated by an almost wilfully bad diet and excessive drinking. By the early 1990s, he was all but destitute, living in cheap motels or charity hostels, apparently through with making music, and subsisting on the meagre proceeds of the classical music LPs that he scavenged from Salem, Oregon, thrift stores and sold to collectors. (As a dedicated thrift-store scavenger myself, I always found this now-accepted stitch in the Fahey mythos a bit suspect. Even if the economics made sense – which they don't – classical music collectors in the 1990s were getting *rid* of their old vinyl and converting en masse to digital technology. If precedent is anything to go by, it's more likely that Fahey was sponging off some girlfriend or ex-wife.)

A celebratory 1994 profile in *Spin* magazine brought Fahey back to public attention; before long, one of rock music's unlikelier comebacks was under way. Fresh new fans flocked to him, duplicating, in a slightly spooky way, Fahey's own fraught 1960s experiences with Skip James and other sacred old monsters of the blues. Young enthusiasts turned up at Fahey gigs expecting some approximation of the sublime sound-worlds of his late-1960s work; what they found, more often than not, was a grumpy, ungainly, and frequently inebriated middle-aged guy in poor health, terrible clothes, and high umbrage. Fahey could be surly and petulant; the neat, stork-like figure from old photos was now an elective slob decked out in stained T-shirts, roomy shorts, and cheap, audience-blocking sunglasses. Requests for old favourites were met with howls of migrainous feedback and long passages of monochromatic drone music.

For Fahey, this switch in musical styles seemed to constitute a grand heroic gesture. He claimed to be bored with his classics, insisting that they were a gigantic act of bad faith ('cosmic sentimentalism') to begin with. Art should be a scream from the gut, not a pretty but devious sublimation: this was his new psycho-aesthetic line. Did he really believe this, or was it merely a face-saving rationalization for the uncomfortable truth that he could no longer perform his chimingly complex 1960s material? Some who were close to Fahey in his final years felt that he was avoiding the fact that he could no longer navigate those long-gone ragas and suites; others believe that Fahey felt he had to give a spiky young audience something appropriately 'radical.' Paradoxically, the spiky young audience found his aping of en vogue drone music a bit second-hand and would have vastly preferred the redemptive beauty of his older music. Also, some of us were kinder than we might have been when reviewing the new CDs that Fahey released during this time; the truth is, the music they contain is not a patch on his best work.

To complicate an already ambiguous situation, Fahey published a quasi-memoir in 2000, in which he accused his father of concerted and vicious child abuse. He had ignored the pain of this memory for far too long, he said; it was also why he considered his gorgeous 60s and 70s music a cop-out, made in psychological bad faith. (Oddly enough, or maybe not, a Fahey compilation from 1994 bore the title *Return of the Repressed*.) Muddying things even further, the book was a foggy mix of half-veiled memory, recalled fantasy, and actual fiction. (It should be noted that in the 1980s and 1990s, so-called satanic-abuse scandals and the controversial area of 'recovered memories' were both hot topics.) The truth behind Fahey's suddenly sprung abuse narrative remains opaque – and, finally, depressing, either way. Before assembling his score-settling memoir, he doesn't seem to have hinted at the existence of such problems to anyone – friend, partner, or family member. As with Fahey's maybe-daring, maybe-lazy turn toward drone music, old fans remain split on the subject; some feel that the horrific revelations seemed suspiciously well-timed to excuse his own bad behaviour.

Indeed, Fahey appears to have been a fairly unbearable character in his last years. (He died aged 61, in 2001, from complications while undergoing heart surgery.) Here we find a type familiar from numerous rock biographies: the lazy-but-controlling middle-aged child who expects everything to be done for him as his seignorial due, helpless when faced with necessary change but mule-like in clinging to entrenched habit – and cloaked in recherché sexual politics. Toward the close of the Lowenthal biography (the only one so far), we find an unsettling example of Fahey bestowing attentions on a young female fan that feels just short of stalking. Late Fahey is one of those divisive figures whose personal behaviour can seem as petty and self-serving as his best music is otherworldly and sublime. It may be hard to still enjoy the work of old (usually male) heroes once we learn about the recurrence of some worse-than-usual moral laxity. (Allegations that the late electro-folkie John Martyn may have been a periodic wife-beater have ruined his impossibly gentle music for many ex-fans.) But in some cases, we may find that an artist's perplexingly messy life only increases our awe before the rough beauty of their work. Music, we may suppose, is the one place where these grossly imperfect souls glimpse or brush against the hopeful lineaments of a better life.

Adult temper tantrums and disabling drug habits are depressingly familiar stuff in musicians' biographies; in Fahey's case, aspects of his bad behaviour might betray a deeper resonance. Fahey's contemporaries in the folk revival were ethically unimpeachable, but their music was the proverbial last straw that sent you to watch paint dry instead. Is it better to endure bad art for the spotless ideology it promotes, or to continue to swoon before sublime art made by awful people?

As for Fahey's own sublime art, much of his back catalogue is being reissued on vinyl again. It continues to ensnare astonished new listeners – some not even born when Fahey died – hungry for a folk music that is convincingly delicate and diabolic both, never winsome or pompous or plain. Many of these new fans are the age I was in 1979, when Fahey was one of the first music people I interviewed professionally. Back then, I couldn't quite believe that we were even in the same room. If I had known how the word was used, I would probably have called him 'maestro'. He was polite, garrulous, and arrestingly articulate on a wide range of musical and extra-musical topics.

From small cottage-industry beginnings to a punk-era fade and then post-grunge rediscovery and his egregious child-abuse controversy, Fahey's career took an oddly emblematic trajectory for such a superficially modest life. The Fahey I met in London in 1979 was tweedy and professorial, calm and sanguine, and helpful almost to a fault. In his twilight years, he was more like some dodgy backstreet character you might see in a dull episode of *Cops*. Latter-day Fahey could seem both a wan and forbidding figure: lost inside his grey rainbow haze of prescription meds and phantom ailments, fast food and concerted drift, claiming psychological dysfunction almost as a badge of honour. He seemed to fritter away what little energy he had left in various forms of bad-tempered self-sabotage. Something had happened in Fahey's world, and it felt more elemental than just a bad case of chronic fatigue. The coexistence of the abuse narrative with his increasing borderline abuse of the women in his life may hold a key. Other problems may have begun as early as the late 1960s: his surprising *Easy Rider*-style commercial success drew in its train agents, ideologues, and 'underground' sibyls seeking a supplementary message or profit from a music never built to withstand such subtle but muddling imprecations. He had set out to do something winningly simple, and it had gotten very complicated indeed.

It's sad, hearing all these murky refrains from a life that went intermittently wrong toward its premature end; but I can't say that, after such knowledge, my favourite Fahey albums sound any less magical now. His best work has a beguiling melancholy but is never depressing, wistful but never facile. Fahey is just one man surveying the tradition and leaving his thumbprint on its originary manuscripts, an impression so rapt and easy and unassuming that it might be breath or breeze. Newcomers consulting the Lowenthal biography may wonder why the author chose the rather glum *Dance of Death* as a title rather than *American Guitarist*: the author perhaps overemphasizes the morbid side of Fahey, when a large part of his catalogue is quite rousing and cheerful. (A good percentage of blues music did, after all, start life as a wholly intemperate, Saturday-night get-down beat.) In the end, 'American' is surely the most telling and accurate label for a music that seems to speak, inimitably, of both glorious possibilities and misplaced Edens. John Fahey may have ended his life a spoiled and irascible baby-man, but his greatest work continues to resonate for many of us like the ultimate lost chord, deep inside.

SO HIP IT HURTS: STEELY DAN'S
DONALD FAGEN LOOKS BACK

In January 1974, Joni Mitchell released the exquisite, deceptively sunny *Court and Spark*; two months later, on the penultimate day of March, the Ramones played their first gig. The year obviously had some fine diversions and big surprises in store for the clued-up rock fan. But if you had to identify a dominant trend that year, it was huge stadiums echoing to the roar of monumentally heavy boogie. A lot of endless, finesse-free jamming. A lot of stack-heeled get-down. A job lot of stretched-thin double-live albums. A brutalized 12-bar blues without end.

Donald Fagen and Walter Becker sat uneasily in this world of earnest sentiment and antediluvian riffing. An impassively odd couple with encyclopaedic jazz smarts and a glowering, gnomic mien, in some ways they sat exactly midway between Joni and the Ramones: pinup idols of the urbane Los Angeles studio scene but with bags of spiky, shades-after-midnight New York City attitude.

Dorm buddies who met at Bard College in upstate New York, Becker and Fagen started out in a band called the Bad Rock Group, with Chevy Chase, no less, on drums. They were over-literate beatniks with mid-night-cafeteria tans and their own slinky, Beat-derived argot. Their second band found its name courtesy of William Burroughs: Steely Dan 111 is a garrulous sex aid, a minor player in the fizzing mind/body loop of *Naked Lunch*. Musically, the Dan were more jazz-inflected than rock-driven, filled out by a movable feast of session musician pals. For their debut single, they picked 'Do It Again', a baleful lament about finding nothing new under the sun. At a time when sitars played as prettily exotic signifiers of limpid bliss, they amped one up for a biting, nerve-jangled solo. At a time when *Rolling Stone* ran long, fawning Q & As with addled vocalists and the counterculture was sold on faux revolutionary emblems, Becker and Fagen essayed a light samba to declare that it was all bunk: 'A world become one, of salads and sun? Only a fool would say that.'

Putting the hook up front, taking things easy, capering along to the prevailing ethos – none of this was the Steely Dan way. Even so, 1974's *Pretzel Logic* felt like the oddest work of an already odd career. The front cover gave little away – a monochrome shot, school of Winogrand or Arbus, of a New York street-food vendor. The title track is a surreal roadhouse blues, which switches lanes into an awed reverie on Napoleonic hubris. Other songs are gossamer light, over in a minute or two, like demos that a more popular act rejected for being too spectral, morbid, tart.

Becker and Fagen started out as songwriter hacks for hire, pale ghosts in the all-business Brill Building. 'Through with Buzz', 'Charlie Freak', 'With a Gun': a rough sketch of how hit singles might sound in some spooky alternate universe. Chart hits that got lost in a notorious park one night or missed civics class to stay in bed and read Henry Miller. As if to prove the point, Steely Dan then scored the biggest hit of their career with 'Rikki Don't Lose That Number', a hesitant, mnemonic in-joke, strung around the card-shuffle chord changes of jazz pianist Horace Silver's 'Song for My Father'. To date, it remains the only chart smash that kicks off with an unaccompanied, 23-second marimba solo.

But the strangest confection on a strange menu may

have been their retooling of Duke Ellington's 1927 composition 'East St Louis Toodle-Oo'. It sits at the end of what we used to call Side One, as the real-life East St Louis sits on one side of the Mississippi, facing the slightly tonier St Louis. Ellington's original is a lilting chameleonic vamp, perfect accompaniment for a pleasure cruise down the River Styx. It starts out mournful as recollected sin (you can see the bowed heads, the black frocks snaking behind a stately hearse), but then the dark clouds disperse and the band starts to raise everyone's knees, as if to prove that succour and sunshine were hiding under the heart-sore funk all along. It sounds in two minds – sad and ornery, yet elegantly drunk – and ends where it began, Bubber Miley's trumpet growling like a hungry bear.

Becker and Fagen take their own 'Toodle-Oo' at a slightly brisker clip, as though they're downing cheap champagne on a fast train home from the funeral. They usher in some unexpected guests to the wake: willowy pedal steel, gravelly wah-wah guitar, and tingling stride piano replace the two-toned horns of the original. 'Toodle-Oo' 2.0 shouldn't work, but does; shouldn't swing, but really does. It feels deeply affectionate, not glib. Steely Dan were later sampled, in their turn, by thrusting young hip-hop acts: wheel turning round and round. Nothing on *Pretzel Logic* is overstressed or overplayed; it's seriously hip but devilishly playful. 'Parker's Band' may slip in clever nods to certain Charlie Parker titles ('You'll be groovin' high or relaxin' at Camarillo'), but primarily it duplicates the joy of being floored by a polyphonic bebop rush for the first time. The drums are a rising heartbeat; when a multitracked squall of saxophones blows in without warning, you may want to rise and offer your own syncopated hallelujahs.

130

Still, many pop/rock fans were suspicious and remain so to this day. For the doubters, Steely Dan personified the infamous Terry Southern put-down: 'You're too hip, baby! I just can't carry you.' Even Dan fans started to read the work as if it was one big put-on – a prophylactic, perhaps, against the real pain and melancholy that some of these songs contained. Maybe all along, it was the audience that was too hip, not the band; there was definitely a stripe of intellectual snobbery among would-be acolytes like my teenage self. Other spoiled rock superstars maybe 'didn't give a fuck about anyone else' (in the words of 'Show Biz Kids') because they were empty-headed snots; if Becker and Fagen also didn't, we Dan fans agreed, it was coming from a far better, or wiser – or maybe a far crueller – place.

Some of this cognitive dissonance may be attributable to the fact that the more critics fawned over Steely Dan, the more the duo responded with markedly blasé gratitude. It may also be due to the palette they were drawing on – precedents such as Broadway theatre, soundtrack scoring, West Coast jazz. These were traditions in which a big production number didn't necessarily mean what it said; smiling major chords disclosed drooling wolf fangs; and a desolate blues prepared the soil for subsequent flags of triumph. It's hipness of a different order – tone and texture matter as much as, if not more than, what is explicitly said or sung. (In an early interview, Fagen claimed he was amazed that anyone liked his singing at all, when it sounded, he averred, like a 'Jewish Bryan Ferry'.) The Dan's variety of minor-chord legerdemain went against the prevailing mid-70s grain, an ethos where every precious singer-songwriter word was presumed to be heartfelt.

But then, Steely Dan went against the grain in a

number of ways. They relocated to Los Angeles in pursuit of superior recording technology, but didn't really fit the local scene. In a press shot for 1980's *Gaucho*, the duo look like creatures just emerged from a long and difficult hibernation; their flesh has the same grey, drained, plasma hue as the bony hands of the album's cover art. Becker could be a backstreet physician, on the lam in a cheap hippie wig; Fagen looks like the anorexic, smart-ass kid brother of Jeff Goldblum's *Fly* guy. Rumours began to surface of Steely Dan giving Fleetwood Mac a run for their per diem, as far as deepwater dysfunction and high-end narcotics. The difference was that the Dan's decadence felt more oblique and therefore more tantalizing – these were chord-progression wonks, not boogie ogres! There was an added frisson in the idea of these two cerebral New Yorkers adrift in scented-candle lotusland, like a modern-day Bird and Prez. Soon enough, they did both crash and burn, in discrete ways, and a long sabbatical followed. They packed up and left Los Angeles. Becker negotiated a divorce from his five-fathom drug habit in sunny Hawaii. Fagen returned to New York and, by his own account, embraced a long-postponed, full-bore breakdown.

There was never any point when Dan devotees felt: here are two guys who might open up and let us in on the odd-couple arrangement, all the extracurricular accidents and emergencies. They were never at the top of any list you'd draw up of people who would one day pen heartfelt memoirs about their lives in music. And while I can't see it getting an approving Oprah sticker, the big surprise about *Eminent Hipsters* is that it turns out to be, after a fashion, just that: Donald Fagen's heartfelt memoir. Sure, he hides the fact behind a spunkily disingenuous 'it just fell together' introductory gloss, but it's still more flesh-and-blood affecting than even the craziest Dan watcher might have dreamed. This being Donald Fagen, he doesn't come right out and solicit for big redemptive group hugs; the more tender lines are well hidden behind his deceptively offhand writing style. The first half is a suite of essays rooted in the late 50s and early 60s concerning 'artists whose origins lay outside the mainstream': forgotten singers, arrangers, sci-fi crazies, ahead-of-the-curve DJs and tastemakers. This brief takes in the overlooked Boswell Sisters; the underpraised – and arguably overdemonized – Ike Turner; and the quietly influential real-life nightfly DJs Mort Fega and Jean Shepherd. Fagen also offers a few personal reflections on his late teenage years. The second half, 'With the Dukes of September', is a diary he kept in 2010 while touring with Boz Scaggs and Michael McDonald.

While the essays present a fascinating prospect, the tour diary looks like it might be a bad goof, a parody of old-time rock-star self-indulgence. Who needs it, even from one-half of Steely Dan? Do we want cool guys to spill? Doesn't our fascination rest precisely on their flinty, recessive nature? But 'With the Dukes' turns out to be one of the laugh-out-loud funniest things anyone ever penned about the workaday woes of being a pro musician. It's such outrageous fun, in fact, that it threatens to overshadow the less showy virtues of the essays. Structurally, the book doesn't quite hang together: it feels like two different pitches jammed together to make one awkward hybrid. If *Eminent Hipsters* were a film, you can imagine a weave of the two strands: jaded, lost-in-America Donald has a series of flashback reveries while spaced out along the tour, recalling just how it was that young Donny got here and who inspired him to light out this way.

There are moments when, exploring twenty-first-century America, Fagen has cause to both revisit his own chequered past and re-evaluate some of his heroes. There's a mildly tragicomic episode where Fagen realizes that he is to play a local auditorium named after Count Basie. His mood brightens – and then darkens after he realizes that none of the audience seem to know, or care, who this blow-in foreigner Count Basie is, anyway. Fagen doesn't belabour the point, but it might be a good topic for a social studies class: What is the point of civic commemoration if you're commemorating a blank? *Eminent Hipsters* may itself be Fagen's way of throwing a greasy spanner into the works, at a moment when Steely Dan seem to be settling nicely into rock's own nostalgic industry. Fagen scans the American hinterland and wonders what he's doing and whether a creaking, picky New York homebody should be doing it at all at his age. Do the 'TV babies', as he calls younger consumers (a phrase out of Allen Ginsberg via Gus Van Sant's 1989 *Drugstore Cowboy*), even know why he's honouring the old R & B pioneers whose ghosts he calls up nightly? Has the public conversation gone stone-cold dead?

Fagen doesn't want to come across like one of those testy old cranks who get aggrievedly reactionary with age ('Hobbesian geezers' – a nice bit of phrase making), but he doesn't want to kid himself that all is right with the world, either. What he wants is some kind of safe, hallowed, but still-testing middle ground. He recalls the often derided era of the early 60s as a time with its own sense of verve, jest, and decorum. Of that era's TV: 'lots of swell black-and-white movies from the 30s and 40s, all day and most of the night. No soul-deadening porn or violence. Decent news programs and casual entertainment featuring intelligent, charming celebrities like Steve Allen, Groucho Marx, Jack Paar, Jack Benny, Rod Serling, and Ernie Kovacs.' For a flinty old cynic, he can be suasively rhapsodic: 'And I'll start thinking about a late summer sun setting over fifteen hundred identical rooftops and my family and bop glasses and Holly Golightly, about being lonesome out there in America and how that swank music connected up with so many things.'

It's a portrait of the artist as an embryonic Florida retiree: grumpy, fidgety, fond (his hotel room iPod plays nothing but old Verve jazz or Stravinsky), ungrateful toward fans, snarling at managers, leering at young poolside babes, spiteful to hotel staff. Fagen doesn't skirt the risk of deep mortification. He leads us round 360 degrees of his touring profile: petty, grouchy, backward-looking, too smug by half. And yet, while it appears to be an entirely truthful account, all the time part of me was thinking: Is this actually the equivalent of a well-crafted Steely Dan character? 'Deacon Blues' on Prozac? As I said to a friend and fellow Dan obsessive, *Eminent Hipsters* is essentially *On the Road* with Alvy Singer. In Woody Allen's *Annie Hall* (1977), his OCD doppelgänger Singer loathes Los Angeles, but work and romance install him there for months at a time. Allen initially wanted to name his feel-good comedy after a bleak psychiatric diagnosis: anhedonia, a condition that also seems to cover how Fagen now feels about touring: 'The inability to experience pleasure from activities usually found enjoyable.' Like Allen, Fagen seems deeply versed in the language of shrinks and footnotes from the *Physicians' Desk Reference*. In the missing years between *The Nightfly* and resumption of his partnership with Becker, Fagen had a real Freudian schlep of therapy, and much (legal) pharmaceutical rewiring. While you still wouldn't call him a little ray of sunshine, these efforts seem to have done a lot to revamp his subsequent life: marriage, uninterrupted work, a relative cessation of hostilities with the media. While the younger Donald might conceivably have *written* a tour diary, you can't imagine he would have allowed it to be published.

Today, when we identify a hipster, it carries entirely different connotations from the word's original, darkly lustrous charge. 'Hipster' is now a slight, because hipsters now are slight – not so much a soulful tribe as a fly-eyed pose looking for somewhere to land. Hipsters move into your locale, and before you know it, brittle quotation marks are strung everywhere. Hipsters have become little more than an advance guard for the arcadia of 'hip capitalism'. Once, though, it truly mattered how hip you were. In Fagen's day, things were different. Born in 1948, he belongs to a baby-boomer generation for whom the benediction of hip was most devoutly to be desired. It was a dark and uncertain thing, an arduous rite of passage, almost a spiritual gamble. Lewis MacAdams, in his 2001 overview, *Birth of the Cool: Beat, Bebop, and the American Avant-Garde*, recalls how New York bohemian Judith Malina (later cofounder of the Living Theatre) found herself briefly jailed following a mid-Manhattan protest march. A nice middle-class girl under it all, she's shocked to find herself sharing space with honest-to-goodness streetwalkers. 'I like you,' declaims one prisoner to Malina, 'but let's face it. You're a square.' MacAdams supplies a subtle but powerful sense of where hip's true cargo originates. If it's at street level, the street is on the other side of town. Hip was, most of all, a black phenomenon, 'cool in its slavery-born sense, where attitude and stance is the only self-defence against overwhelming rage'.

New York was the seedbed of hip: Harlem's Apollo, Birdland, the Cedar Tavern, the *Village Voice*. Hipness was arcane. If you had to ask, you were nowhere. MacAdams: 'Everything had to be understated, circuitous, metaphorical, communicated in code.' It was a time when drugs of any kind, interracial dalliance, homosexual love, could all earn you serious jail time. Then, as the 60s loomed, hip slithered into the mainstream light: it began to be discussed, analysed, advertised. A lot of blame should probably be placed at Norman Mailer's door. True hipsters would let slip one pithy phrase or exit inside a ringing Zen ellipsis; Mailer blathered on at great length and made hipsterism seem verbose, fraudulent, a cheap thrill for bored socialites. He missed the unmissable point, which was: never explain or sermonize. There was an art to betraying nothing in public – not anger or fear, approval or approbation. Cool manners were a shield for those who were allowed few weapons of self-defence, a ghetto hijack of Kipling's 'If you can keep your head when all about you are losing theirs', both mask and recompense for folks who had a justified feeling that all sweet ideological promises tended to leave them in the same dreadful hole, holding the sharp end of the stick.

Fagen's roll call of hipsterdom doesn't promote some overfamiliar cast of scurvy Beats and angry savants, bemoaning the plastic tragedy of conformist Amerikkka. Fagen *likes* plastic. He digs people who straddle the divide between hep and square, margin and MOR, a no-man's zone where apparent squares take on the prompts of hip and parlay them into a wider audience. 'The concept of hip had exploded into the culture in a new manifestation.' Fagen is very good on artists from that time (Basie and Ellington, Erroll Garner, Billy Eckstine, Sarah Vaughan) who, abandoned by the hipster cognoscenti, worked their way into less cool but far more secure and remunerative positions. Most were in the early autumn of long careers, and while they weren't up for stretching any more boundaries, they could still knock out work of devastating economy and depth. Fagen's paradigm is not the supposedly world-changing works like *Howl* or *On the Road*, Ornette Coleman's *Free Jazz*, or Stanley Kubrick's *Dr Strangelove* – it's concertedly in-between stuff, bronchial guys in airless studios fussing over augmented chord progressions. Fagen is lyrical about his idol Ray Charles – hobbled by racism, blindness, and addiction, but a canny operator who smooched the mainstream with roughed-up textures, surprising combinations, dissimulated taunts. In another lovely tribute, 'Henry Mancini's Anomie Deluxe', Fagen explains how the eponymous arranger used jazz idioms and jazz players in his TV and film work. 'He utilized the unconventional, spare instrumentation associated with the cool school: French horns, vibraphone, electric guitar and – Mancini's specialty – a very active flute section, including both alto flute and the rarely used bass flute. Instruments were often individually miked to bring out the detail... There was a lot of empty space. It was real cool.' Mancini gave a bop edge to such TV bagatelles as *Peter Gunn* and *Mr Lucky*, just as Quincy Jones would later score *Ironside* and pianist Lalo Schifrin would rework the unforgettable *Man from U.N.C.L.E.* theme. (Both Schifrin and Jones were graduates of the Dizzy Gillespie touring band, and Jones was

138

mentored early on by Ray Charles.) Mancini titles such as 'Dreamsville' and 'A Profound Gass' (*sic*) inspired Fagen to learn more about jazz, and 'out of these fragments of hip and hype I constructed in my mind a kind of Disneyland of Cool'. For a moment, we're dropped into the adolescent Donald's reverie about a Mancini recording session: 'Everybody's smoking Pall Malls or some other powerful nonfilter cigarettes. Hank hands out the parts. When they run down the chart, a thick membrane of sound flows forth and hovers in the room. It sounds incredibly plush.' It's rare to read a musician who writes so well about the recording process.

Shelves of books are devoted to unearthing the fugitive 'meaning' of pretty song lyrics, yet often it's some forgotten scrap of melody that cracks us apart; an old sitcom theme from decades ago can deep-six us more effectively than most big-name, chart-topping tracks. Becker and Fagen knew all about the occult effectiveness of tone and texture. The more studio time they could afford, the more they explored this world of sonic spacing, layering, and counterpoint. Across *Aja* and *Gaucho* and Fagen's own *Nightfly*, musical grain counts as much as buffed-up words. Listen again to 'Black Cow' from *Aja*: a moony relationship, bogged down in slackness and routine. Recrimination rears its snapping-turtle head, and breakup is surely imminent: 'I can't cry any more / While you run around.' The rhythm uncurls like someone under deep anaesthetic. Plod, plod, plod, through a big black cloud. Then ('just when it seems so clear') we turn a corner and the music perks up, becomes almost punch-the-sky joyous, a homecoming parade of high-five bass and pungent roadhouse sax.

Or try 'New Frontier' from *The Nightfly*, which opens with an ear-popping surge of forward motion. Drums skip and skim like speedboats leaving a summer jetty; the electric piano nudges you with a conspiratorial grin. The chorus rises and falls like sun motes on a holiday balcony. But there's something else here, under all the mist and spray – a strange hesitant guitar fill, like a nagging second thought, fussing away throughout the song. The major-chord whole is so effervescent and pulls you along in such a happy trance that it's only in retrospect that you realize what a difficult balancing act Fagen pulls off. In 'New Frontier', he distils the secret fears slumbering under the aquamarine repose of hot summertime fun. Fagen sounds upbeat, like a Supremes 45, but 'the key word is survival on the new frontier'. Take that how you will. In isolation, it has a ring of tooth-and-claw realpolitik. But survival is living, too, and in the end, 'New Frontier' is a low-down limbo shimmy, celebrating a new-dawn limbo time.

The song's title is an uncharacteristically candid reference to an antecedent text: John F. Kennedy's speech accepting his presidential nomination at the 1960 Democratic convention. The onset of the decade ahead: Camelot dawning, and Kennedy eternally young and forever tan in blinky monochrome footage. When the women behind him applaud, all you can see is a blur of white dress gloves. The New Frontier was a tiny nugget phrase that set free outsize reverberations. From 'IGY', which launches *The Nightfly*: 'Standing tough under stars and stripes / We can tell: this dream's in sight.' But consult the speech in question, and you find that it has a surprisingly ashy Cold War taste. Rather than the expected sound-barrier boom of celebration, the message is more like: *ignore this advice at your peril.* The speech's rhetorical march falls on a series of hesitant downbeats: 'unknown', 'unfilled', 'uncharted', 'unsolved',

'unconquered', 'unanswered'. It's full of pinched undertones, as much provocation as celebration. Are you up to
the trek ahead? Have you got the bright stuff? Do you
relish the idea of uncharted space, unfilled time? As
much as he was looking forward, celebrating American
know-how and optimism, Kennedy was also speaking
against unacknowledged failings: prejudice, poverty,
everything that held the American Dream out of reach
for many sections of post-war US society. On the page, if
you Magic-Marker those via-negativa *un*words, it looks
like the grand bummer of all New Tomorrow speech-
es, and a less capable speaker might have stumbled
and missed his moment. JFK had a rather nasal, whiny
voice, but boy, could he deliver a lyric. He was the Bob
Dylan of 60s political oratory.

Fagen's original hipster era is now as old-world distant and faraway as a Victorian player piano or, indeed,
the urtext that Fagen swipes his own title from: Lytton
Strachey's 1918 study, *Eminent Victorians*. Strachey
caused a big stir with his discreetly anti-hagiographical
work, but he saw this slim volume as a resource as much
for future readers as for his own contemporaries. Lytton
was a bit of a proto-hipster himself – beardy, polysexual, equally at home with Maynard Keynes or sheaves of
fussy French Symbolist poetry. Where Strachey was out
to puncture received wisdom about the era in question,
Fagen wants to rescue a misunderstood time. Just possibly, Fagen has something similar in mind to Strachey's
idea of a biographical time capsule – he may be writing
against his time, as much as for it. (The diary form is
a useful means of raising serious concerns in a deceptively airy manner.) Looked at in this way, the essays
seem less of an ad-hoc grab bag. A quick glimpse at the

table of contents may suggest that Fagen's essay choices are flagrantly, even perversely, personal; but they add up to an overview of a specific historical moment. As MacAdams puts it in *Birth of the Cool*: 'Before, there had been many individual acts of cool. Now Cool – a way, a stance, a knowledge – was born.' Previously, what was hip had been the preserve of certain underground cliques, signalling among themselves in the darkness. Most of all, black American culture in general and jazz culture in particular were the choppy currents that fed into societal sea change.

Hip now found itself working backup for – not the Man exactly, but close enough. Fagen is spot-on identifying hip's undercover dispersal through phenomena like TV cop shows, the film version of *Breakfast at Tiffany's*, and Sinatra's pals in the Rat Pack. Here were 'street-wise swingers' who were palpably hip, 'but they could operate in the straight world with existential efficiency'. This birthed a tradition of what you might call 'straight hip', exemplified by the one guy Lalo Schifrin worked for more than anyone else: Clint Eastwood. Starting with his own nightfly DJ character in *Play Misty for Me*, through the imperturbably cool (and sharply dressed) Harry Callahan, Eastwood embedded discreetly hip tones in precariously conservative settings, right up to *Bird*, his controversial 1988 biopic of original hipster Charlie Parker. Perhaps none of this should surprise us. The conventional wisdom about the success of something like *Mad Men* is that it plays to our cloudy nostalgia for a time before political correctness and the culture wars, a time when we were positively encouraged to smoke and exist on a diet of highballs, one-night stands, and diet pills. Everything free and easy, no constant checking of guidelines (and e-mails).

But isn't this nostalgia less for a lax, ring-a-ding time than for a lost grid, where every moral choice was mapped out? Where everyone accepted the existence of common rules? After all, frontiers are places where things end as well as begin. It's all about a pleasurable tension between strict rules and raised-eyebrow rule breaking. Think of Eastwood as Callahan. He's got swell loafers and perfect shades, but he's thin red line to the core. He swings – but not in front of the children, or on the streets, or for public consumption. I suspect that in decades to come, people will be absolutely baffled by the high-colour moral variegation of the *Dirty Harry* series.

Rule breaking is only worthwhile when the rules you break have real meaning. Fagen is funny but acute on that moment in our teenage years when we snub parents and dismiss all authority figures but simultaneously initiate a desperate search for persuasively hep figures, people to tell us exactly what we should listen to, view, and read. What to *dig*. The mainstream culture of that early-60s era may get a bad rap for being queasily paternalistic, but sometimes we need experts to teach us the art of making fine distinctions and keeping valuable traditions alive. Our twenty-first-century snake-oil promise of 'more choice' often devolves into homogeneous slop, a moraine of thin and stony repetition. In the current YouTube moment, we're told that we have a limitless look-see option on everything there ever was, laid out right before us – but at the price, perhaps, of a complete absence of critical chiaroscuro. Look up Steely Dan's wistful 'Hey Nineteen' on Wikipedia, and you find: 'See also: Age disparity in sexual relationships.' Which is nearly straight-faced inapt enough to be a Becker–Fagen in-joke.

Hipsters these days have to use all their desperate

wiles just to stay one step ahead of the local TV news; but back in Fagen's youth, sources of alternative info were next to zero. It's easy to sneer at the old idea of 'in the know' hepcats, but hipsters once really were those who lit out for terra incognita. I have deeply ambivalent feelings about the over-canonized Beats, but it's easy to forget the reason they were elected figureheads in the first place: they sallied forth into the unknown and set about indexing the whole of American dreaming, not just a few choice, sanitized cuts. Some of their takes on black culture may now strike us as risible and patronizing, and some of the quasi-religious holy-fool sub-notes feel a bit self-hypnotized (and on, and on); but at the time, they were navigating wholly without maps.

There are times on his grand tour of the US in 2010 when Fagen wonders if a whole lot has changed over the preceding 50 years. There may be a black president, but whole swathes of culture are in danger of being reforgotten, belittled, or neutered in divisive 'culture wars' (with errors of taste and scale on both sides). He's alternately combative and perplexed: a 63-year-old singing the golden notes of his youth and struggling to work out if they still mean anything – if any songs do. In the end, Fagen is hip enough to know that you can't run from your own adult quandaries. There are deeply affecting passages here about family and marriage, loss and ageing – things the younger Donald might not have copped to: difficult negotiations, real blues. When you've spent your life using Cool to hold an untidy, insensate world at bay, how do you manage the rough stuff when it rears up and blindsides you on the street where you live, one fine day?

He's good on his parents – both 'the father thing' and

a mother who was a more than capable lounge singer, far more creative than she let on (and thus emblematic of many women from that era with curtailed dreams). Fagen senior was someone who sincerely believed in the promise of the American Dream but found himself knocked to the canvas by real economic jabs. There was the rhetorical fandango of JFK's New Frontier, and then there was how it played out in workplaces, bank accounts, and parental bedrooms. Also, you begin to see where the askew texture of Steely Dan lyrics may have found some of its everyday inspiration: his parents lived in a 'nightmarishly bland apartment, which was in a high-rise building on – wait for it – Chagrin Boulevard'. Finally, Fagen's hipster is not what Anita Brookner, in a lovely spearing of Baudelaire, called a Propagandist of the *Pauvre Moi*. What's revealing about the scattered reflections in *Eminent Hipsters* is that, in the end, the claim that Fagen makes for these marginal eminences is that they were *good people*. Good for art, good for the social fabric, good examples for one and all.

In those long-gone, fake-ID years, the other Donald longed to be a night-blessed pulp-fiction character with a cynical blonde on his arm and big thoughts in his nodding head. 'That shape is my shade / There where I used to stand.' Well, he got his dream. In the same way Bob Dylan has slowly become one of those gravel-voiced old troubadours he started out imitating, Fagen is now a prickly old jazzer, languid and bittersweet. Still on the road, still making for the border, still so hip it hurts. Next March, it will be 40 years since *Pretzel Logic*: the same interval as between Ellington's merciful 'Toodle-Oo' and the Dan's own fizzing but seemly tribute. Some frontiers never grow old.

THE QUESTION OF U: THE MIRROR
IMAGE OF PRINCE

'Assiduously and without much constraint,
he conditioned his personality, making it as
impenetrable and resourceful, as submissive and
difficult, as it had to be for the sake of his mission.'
—— Walter Benjamin, 'The Image of Proust'

'To create in myself a nation with its own politics,
parties and revolutions, and to be all of it, everything,
to be God in the real pantheism of this people-I'
—— Fernando Pessoa, *The Book of Disquiet*

'It is the first or Christian name that counts, that is
what makes one be as they are.'
—— Gertrude Stein, writing about Ulysses S. Grant

1.

In autumn 1981, hot new act Prince was offered two
nights at the Los Angeles Memorial Coliseum supporting the Rolling Stones. His initial impulse was to turn
them down flat. The Stones had a new album (*Tattoo
You*) to plug and the supporting tour would eventually
bring in $50m in ticket sales, the largest US gross that
year. Still, there was a vague sense that frisky young
Prince – the latest reincarnation of the R'n'B acts the
Stones venerated and in some sense owed their whole
existence to – was being used as a heart-starter, to angry
up these old troupers' thirtysomething blood. As Jason
Draper puts it in *Prince: Life & Times* (2017): 'The average Rolling Stones fan still rode the coattails of 1970s
rock'n'roll, about which everything was neatly defined.
Men played guitars and slept with women, who were

submissive and did what they were told.' In contrast, at this early stage very little about rising star Prince and what he might do next seemed at all 'neatly defined'. But he had his own new album to plug (called, with exact and extrasensory irony, *Controversy*) and owed quite a lot of money – and gratitude – to his label, Warner Brothers: the sales of his previous three albums hadn't met expectations, and there was a feeling that *Controversy* was make or break. In the end, swayed by his hypo-sharp management team, Prince took the gig.

It didn't go well. On the first night, 9 October, Prince and The Revolution barely made it through four songs before getting booed offstage. (Accounts differ, some of them wildly, but it seems to have been one track in particular, 'Jack U Off', that set off most of the derision and homophobic jeers.)[4] The rest of his young band were game to push on, but Prince fled home to Minneapolis in a funk. If he was angry, it was perhaps most of all with himself: at some level he must have suspected something like this might happen. It had been just two years since Disco Demolition Night, when a shock jock and 'anti-disco campaigner' had blown up a crate filled with soul and dance records in front of fifty thousand baseball fans at Chicago's Comiskey Stadium. As the 1980s opened, pop music was still more or less a segregated thing in America.

The second show was scheduled for two nights later, and Prince's manager, his guitarist, even finally Mick

4   Though he was stridently heterosexual, early on Prince got homophobic jeers from both white and black audiences. When the jazz critic Stanley Crouch referred to him as 'the Minneapolis vulgarian and borderline drag queen' as a way of putting down Prince's new pal Miles Davis, it was a public reflection of a lot of private diss.

Jagger himself, all got on the phone to lure the tiny man-diva back. And it worked. But news of the previous flame-out had spread, and the audience came prepared. Prince took to the stage flaunting his trademark look: high-heel boots, thigh-high aerobic stockings and a pair of tight, velvety, minimalist briefs. (He very conspicuously had not opted for a bikini wax.) Apart from a matelot's scarf round his neck, the rest was his lithe, black, naked bod. (For comparison, on this stretch of the tour Mick Jagger mostly wore baggy jerseys representing local American football teams.) The bi-racial, polysexual Revolution likewise came off as a distinctly queer sight in this locale. They were everything that some sections of the LA rock audience despised: disco beats, cross-dressing, New Wave poseurs, aloof and bony synthesizer muzik. The crowd had a collective meltdown. 'Fruit, vegetables, Jack Daniel's bottles, even a bag of rotting chicken came flying through the air at the group,' Draper writes.

In 1981, Prince was an uncomfortable reminder of what lay under the global Good Old Days schtick of the kohl-eyed Stones: an ambiguously inviting/inciting body of colour. Another black innovator stepping up to 'support' another bunch of blithe white minstrels. Many inside Prince's camp saw the Stones gig as a turning point. Already known as something of a control freak, Prince would make sure he was never put in a position like this again – not onstage, not in the media, not in a recording studio, not in any boardroom. He would never again play bottom in this kind of power snuggle.

2.
If Prince had died or disappeared in 1989, he would have left one of the all-time perfect bodies of work. *Dirty Mind*

(1980) to *Lovesexy* (1988): a dazzling yet subtle engagement ring offered to the world. It wasn't until I started on this piece that I remembered how much my own life intertwined with Prince's music throughout the 1980s: I wrote about him more than any other act; I can plot all the high and low points of that shiny/dark hedonistic time using nothing but Prince songs; I attended his first UK gig with the person who was my first serious relationship; by 1987 I'd met, to the endlessly repeated soundtrack of *Sign o' the Times*, the person I was to spend the rest of my life with. Looking at all those perfectly designed album sleeves now is like consulting a set of reverse tarot cards: 'Look! Remember that hotel room in Tangiers...? and that other one in Paris... the shower stall in New York... and so many sunsets, midnights and dawns in long ago North London...' If there is one song that embodies that whole decade for me it's 'If I Was Your Girlfriend': I played it so much it's now something I can't really enjoy any more, simultaneously drained of all meaning and the repository for way too many.

In those glory years Prince was, alongside Madonna, the most fascinating pop star alive. A black R'n'B artist who juggled shiny white pop signifiers; a self-amused imp who made us follow his playfully dense personal mythology from work to work, never knowing what we might find next time round, in what form Prince might return, sometimes mere months later. *Dirty Mind* in no way predicts *Around The World in a Day* (1985), which in no way predicts *Parade* (1986), which sounds nothing like *Lovesexy*. Prince snuck wild swells and shady undercurrents into mainstream pop, with Janus-faced hits like 'When Doves Cry', 'Little Red Corvette' and 'Raspberry Beret'. His first two albums, in the late 1970s, had given no real hint of what was to come. There was a small but crucial element of luck: after that shaky start, it was the deux ex (hit) machina of MTV that was the key, as it was for Madonna and Michael Jackson. For people of a certain age, the lush, melodramatic promo for 'Purple Rain' and the cheeky, pared-down 'Kiss' video are unforgettable.

How did he get away with some of this stuff? *Controversy* came with a full-colour fold-out poster of Prince posing two-thirds naked in the shower. The water drip-drops from his zig-zag briefs; behind him, discreetly positioned on the bathroom wall, is a looming crucifix. On the sleeve of *1999* (1982) he reclines naked like a *Playboy* centrefold, in a neon-dappled boudoir. (His hobbies include horse riding, watercolours and pop eschatology.) On the sleeve of *Dirty Mind* he wears little more than a jacket, those briefs again, and a street hustler's determinedly blank gaze; a tiny black and white badge on his lapel says 'Rude Boy'. (Yes, we see.) Looking back at such images, two things strike you. First, even before Madonna, he was posing himself as an aggressively passive sex object. (These are images that say: 'You think you know whose tongue is in whose cheek, here, but you really don't.') Second, that self-consciously blank gaze, deployed time after time. Look at how expressionless he is in those shots. Has he simply composed his face, or is he wearing it like a mask? Regardless, these early portraits disclose an everyday kid, someone you might see around the neighbourhood, not the flawless no-hair-out-of-place Prince of later years, embalmed inside a pastel armour of good taste, every last bit of skin hidden behind boots, suits, gloves, shades, neo-pimp hats.

I'd completely forgotten, but in these fledgling days there was also a Prince portrait taken by Robert

Mapplethorpe, for *Interview* magazine, in 1980. Surprisingly, it turns out to be the least risqué pic of all: a simple deep focus head and shoulders – if 'simple' is really the right word for this meeting of two such notorious bad boys, at such an ominous and/or propitious moment. There's doubtless much to be said about the scopophilic clinch between Mapplethorpe's downtown eyes and black men's bodies, but the *Interview* portrait is upfront rather than on the downlow, unabashed, full of the 22-year-old Prince's downy and as yet wholly unprocessed personality.

3.
Prince always insisted he was drug-free, but by accident or design his 1980s aesthetic chimed perfectly with the first slowly spreading ripples of Ecstasy in transatlantic pop culture. From *Dirty Mind* to *Around The World* to *Lovesexy* we can map the progress of a new form of pop/soul/other music, ambiguously druggy ('This is not music, this is a trip!') and strangely clear-headed; deliriously erotic but faux naive. Early profiles emphasized an odd mix of confidence and awkwardness: this postmodern Prince was softly spoken, with a tendency to blush; he promised phallic joy but wore thick lisle tights and high-heel boots. His friends and co-workers report how seldom he slept. The result is like something intuited in a lucid late-afternoon dream: 'I was dreaming when I wrote this / Forgive me if it goes astray.' If too many soulful love songs, whatever their merits, are essentially Jack Vettriano, then 1980s Prince was Paul Klee.

The Revolution weren't a classic funk band either, more a sonic Frankenstein welded together in the sort of nightclub where the DJ alternated joy-to-the-world disco and snotty, punch-drunk New Wave. The line-up comprised a geeky white dude in joke-shop doctor's scrubs; a muscly black guy with a dyed mohican; and two strong looking white women of indeterminate sexuality. Prince was having big fun with the play of appearances, abandoning strict reverence to any supposedly 'authentic' truth of what it is to be black, or male, or soulful.

4.

The front sleeve of 'previously unreleased studio recording', *Piano & A Microphone* (recorded 1983, released 2018) is a gorgeous black and white shot of Prince lost in the deeps of his own gaze, in a big dressing room mirror. What do those guarded eyes discern, or foresee? Readers of Lacan may object that the subject seems a bit old to be having any kind of mirror stage moment, but we all know entertainers are a child-like crew who don't grow up at the same rate as the rest of us, if at all. How many future Princes does he see in that reflection, waiting to come out? What does he see there that he's so determined to keep his face blank and give nothing away? You have to wonder: was he trapped inside a wilderness of mirrors, this fatefully curious boy with his nerveless Oedipal eyes? In shots like *Piano & A Microphone*, I sometimes wonder if I see the shuttered gaze of a child who learned at a very young age to never show any too-obvious emotion, to keep things neutral on the domestic battlefront. Look again at that face, made serial on the covers of *Dirty Mind*, *Controversy*, *Purple Rain*: almost wholly without expression. Is it a mask hiding a world of perplexity? Narcissus in search of some missing echo?

From *Dirty Mind* on, there is a definite feeling of some other story under it all: a parallel tale, broody young

Prince off to one side watching himself enact each dutiful role. From the beginning, a double 'you' of two Prince narratives, at least: a public one and a private one; and, echoing between them, a tale which is more to do with race in America, race in the music industry, race where it did or didn't show its face. And it seems to me that this is the subtext missing from a lot of otherwise OK or unexceptionable writing on Prince: the skin game.

Race isn't the only way to make sense of Prince; but to try and make sense of him without it is a truly forlorn hope. Yet, to my knowledge, the only critic who ever tackled this head on is the writer Carol Cooper, an African American woman who also worked in the music industry. In an astute, elegant piece she published in the *Face* in June 1983 (it includes a wholly imaginary Q&A with Prince which was still being quoted as fact three decades later, so acute was her impersonation), Cooper wrote about the way black artists routinely have to 'exaggerate and contort' their image in order to get media coverage. The 'doe-eyed sex freak' was, she notes, just one of many eye-catching constructs the canny Prince used to garner his share of attention.[5]

Cooper had the requisite sense of what black people

5   Listening to *Dirty Mind* again, I was struck by something that sounded like an echo of Van Halen's 'Jump', so looked up the dates. *Dirty Mind*: 1979/80. Van Halen: 1983/84. Now look up the respective entries on Wikipedia. Van Halen get whole paragraphs of technically specific praise – 'driven by a keyboard line, played on an Oberheim OB-X' – and self-glorifying quotes: 'We recut it once in one take for sonic reasons.' Does Prince get similar praise for his far-sighted innovation, for creating the template for so much pop-rock to come? No, he gets one paltry, dismissive phrase: 'demo-like'. Which is typical: reams of purple prose for the latecomer white rockers, while the black artist's risky investment is derided, overlooked or taken for granted.

were still made to go through at that time just to be accepted at all, never mind on a grander, world-conquering scale. She had a beady eye (as Prince did) for the apparently trivial details, coded put-downs and subtle

sightlines of race politics that usually go unmentioned. Black success is different from white – always the extra pressure of having to be a 'role model'. No matter what you do, you never please everyone. If you embrace global success you'll get poison about forgetting your roots; stay close to home and you'll be criticized for lacking ambition. Damned if you do, damned if you don't – as the unruly Rolling Stones gig showed. Prince's black audience had little interest in guitar-led stadium rock anthems; while the rock fans were too hidebound to get that Prince was writing far better songs, and playing far heavier rock, than their profit-eyed, zoned-out heroes.

5.
Prince was born on 7 June 1958 in Minneapolis. His father, John L. Nelson, was 42 at the time; his mother, Mattie Shaw, was 25. His first name was the one his father performed under in a local jazz combo: Prince Rogers. During Prince's formative years it was a volatile household. In one of his biggest hits, 'When Doves Cry', we could be eavesdropping on an analytic session: 'Maybe I'm just like my father, too bold... Maybe I'm just like my mother – she's never satisfied.' A song riven with doubt about loving the other, and the other's love: 'How can you...? Why do we...? Maybe you're...' The story goes that the priapic young Prince was thrown out of his father's house for 'entertaining' girls in the basement music room. And while John Nelson wasn't perhaps as cruelly overbearing as some soul music patriarchs (Marvin

Gaye Snr, Joe Jackson), he seems to have been a man who raised the Bible high at home, but provided enthusiastic musical accompaniment for all the bump'n'grind strippers in the Minneapolis tenderloin.

In early interviews, Prince would tease with hints about his childhood: that his mother showed him *Playboy* magazine in lieu of sex education; that he indulged in near-incest with his half-sister; forever blurring the question of what race he and his parents were, exactly.[6] This was the time of Tipper Gore and her campaign to force record companies to place 'parental warning' stickers on some of their more devil's-spawn LP sleeves. (The kind of dream publicity, it has to be said, most young rock acts dream of.) This sideshow wasn't provoked by some sleazy heavy-metal outrage: the offending party was Prince, and in particular a track called 'Darling Nikki' on the otherwise poptastic *Purple Rain* soundtrack, in which the titular character is found 'in a lobby, masturbating with a magazine'. It's also the only weak song on an otherwise flawless album, a track I routinely skip; even at the time it felt tacky, a self-parodic caricature of the exquisitely economical songs on *Dirty Mind*. Playing *Dirty Mind* now – and this also applies to *1999* and *Purple Rain* – what's really notable is how stark and minimal and unfussy the arrangements sound: Prince had already taken onboard the newfangled synthesizer technology, giving his 'dirty' schtick a rivetingly clean and sprightly sound.

Prince always had a clear idea of where he was headed

6   Prince fudged the issue so much, it was generally reported he had a black father and an Italian mother; in fact his father was black (the family was originally from Louisiana) with a tiny bit of Italian, and Mattie Shaw was a mix of African American, Native American and white.

and the steps that would get him there. He could already write, play, and record entire albums by himself; he then started to have enormous fun with the whole business of stardom, playing his image/persona as if it too was some new kind of synthesiser. This postmodern Prince didn't want fractions of mainstream success, he wanted to be perved over by everyone and their mother; he wanted the cover of *Rolling Stone* as well as an at-home feature in *Jet* magazine.

6.
When I first saw the *Purple Rain* movie in 1984, I thought: what a disaster, this will surely sink him. I was, of course, 100 per cent wrong. It was a classic example of an audience going crazy for something they had no idea they wanted until it was sitting right in front of them. *Purple Rain* was a huge success, delighting Prince's paymasters at Warner Brothers and making future deal-making a lot easier for him. On a symbolic level, *Purple Rain* spun a black overhaul of eternal white movie clichés. Seeded into the ho-hum script were all kinds of lift from Prince's own background: his film mother was played by a Greek actress, Olga Karlatos, muddying further the question of Prince's ambiguous bi-raciality. (It's like a strange negative echo, eighteen years on, from Pete Townshend's 'Substitute' line: 'I look all white / but my dad was black'.)

On the *Purple Rain* soundtrack, 'Let's Go Crazy' is, like the film itself, a spunky celebration of familiar tropes: 'Kids! Don't listen to those ugly straights! They're just jealous of us cool kids!' It's in the music's rainbow sonics that everything is going on here. Prince's voice is set in a frame that's neither straightforward soul music nor rock and roll. It's an elegant hybrid, where clingy opposites attract: acoustic guitar with classical strings on 'Take Me with U'; wobbly church organ with latest-thing synth drums on 'Let's Go Crazy'. In 'The Beautiful Ones' Prince's voice wakes up a sleepy croon, but by song's end it's a mess of jagged shards on the edge of pure noise. We have all heard the epic title track so many times, it's easy to miss how unusual it really is. The opening, casually strummed chords, and the long mournful guitar solo near the end, discreetly call up the ghost of another black psychedelic epic, Funkadelic's 'Maggot Brain'. And rather than ending on a squalling climax, as 99 per cent of rock ballads would, 'Purple Rain' slowly ebbs into nearly two minutes of wistful fugue, until there's only the sound of delicate strings and unfiltered ambient noise. (It's the subcortical memory of details like this which maybe predisposes some of us to find Prince's post-1989 work a bit meh by comparison.)

The success of Purple Rain financed Prince's own Minneapolis studio, Paisley Park, allowing him to build parallel sonic castles in the air. On *Around The World in a Day*, the song 'Paisley Park' refers not to the actual bricks and mortar site, but an imaginary utopia for all his fans around the globe: Prince as would-be Fourier, wrapped in a faux fur ruff. We can see the distance travelled, already, just by comparing the monochrome stare of *Dirty Mind* and, only four years later, the fruit-burst phantasmagoria of *Around The World*, the latter a graphic echo of the insane musical eclecticism inside. It's as if Prince had dared himself to craft a different idiom for all nine songs: pure pop, 1960s Beatles trippiness, 1970s soul man protest – not to mention oddities like 'Tambourine', which only really make sense inside his own swirly world. I still marvel that there was once A Hit Single so sheerly odd as 'Pop Life', and still get an unconscionable amount of pleasure from lines like 'I'm blinded by the daisies in your yard!' from the gorgeous 'Condition of the Heart'. I wasn't entirely sure about all this breathless eclecticism at the time (and the critic in me still goes with *Parade* as his career high), but thirty years on, *Around The World* is the Prince album I play most, for sheer unadulterated pleasure.

If it is mostly sheer pleasure, there are a couple of very odd moments indeed, which suggest that, if you were his 'Beverly Hills shrink', you'd really be earning your fee. 'The Ladder' is a song Prince co-wrote with his father, featuring a royal figure who has to choose between spiritual salvation figured as the title's up-to-the-skies beanstalk, versus his passion for a woman named (ahem) Electra. 'Once upon a time in the land of Sin-a-plenty / there lived a King who didn't deserve to be...' Where to begin with this? Let's just say: if this isn't an inadvertent Lacanian fable about the in-built fragility of the paternal imago, my name is Michael Corleone.

The final track, 'Temptation', features a truly bizarre dialogue about love versus sex, between Prince and (all the signs suggest) God:

G: 'O, silly man, that's not how it works! You have to want it for the right reasons!'
P: 'I do!'
G: 'You don't, now die!'

On this evidence, Prince sounds like a very mixed-up boy indeed, and God (who sounds suspiciously like Prince with his voice pitch-shifted down) is one stern and unforgiving mother – sorry, I mean Father. In retrospect, there's maybe something just a bit queasy about the timing of this – someone young and freaky and black being told by God that he has to die, because of his failure to rein in his sexual promiscuity. But Prince duly promises to 'be good' now that he knows 'love is more important than sex', and then the song (and album) both end on a rather baffling postcard message from someone who's just had one of the biggest hits of the 1980s: 'I have to go now... I don't know when I'll return. Goodbye.'

If that was the final word on *Around The World*, you might be worried for Prince's mortal soul. But the other side of this picture can be found in the video for 'Raspberry Beret', where a grinning Prince looks like he's woken from a grumpy fairy-tale sleep only to realize he's the luckiest boy in the world. Around this time, Prince may well have been one of the happiest people alive, the amount of fun he was having near illegal. A couple of the books under review suggest that the relationship he was in at this point with Susannah Melvoin (twin sister of his bandmate Wendy, and how weird must that have been?) may have been the love of his life. Perhaps not coincidentally, during this period Prince was completely open to collaboration with all-comers, and some quite exquisite work was called forth via the input or inspiration of, among others: Susannah Melvoin, Wendy and Lisa, Matt Fink, and (especially) the marvellous arrangements of jazz guru Clare Fischer.[7]

The whole 1980s catalogue is wonderful, but for me the apotheosis isn't the usual choice, *Sign o' the Times* (1987), but *Parade* (1985). It has everything: joy and

7 Listen to the latter's swooning string arrangement on 'Pink Cashmere' and reflect that this was a 'throwaway' track that only saw the light of day on the *Hits/B-Sides* compilation and was very nearly never heard.

sadness, get-down and wistfulness, mourning and melancholia, group funk and Debussy interludes, echoes of Ellington, Joni, film music, chanson. It's that rare thing among Prince albums: a perfectly realized whole. The opening rush of 'Christopher Tracy's Parade' is breathtaking: strings, trumpets, steel drums, a whole bestiary of strange vibrations swirling around in a quantum funk. A track like 'I Wonder U' is only 1'40" long, but seems to suggest whole new sonic horizons. Looking again at the photo of Prince on the front of *Parade*, I notice how much like a reflection it is: Narcissus before silvered water, examining his features from every sylvan angle, fanning his delicate hands like branches to deflect or direct the light. Turn this mirror-image around on the back cover and his eyes are suddenly shut, the top is coming off, black crucifix exposed. In the great, funny-peculiar and funny-ha-ha video for 'Kiss', Prince poses as the sex object while a seated Wendy steers the song. Fully clothed, amused, powerfully sexy in her own discreet way, Wendy wears the pants, raising a sceptical eyebrow at one point, while a half-naked Prince carries the fantasy. (And who is the strange, veiled, no-gender or bi-gender figure, dancing behind them?)

7.

Sign o' the Times[8] was Prince's attempt to paste together a scrapbook from the wildly various excess of songs that had collected over the previous few years. A devil's advocate critique of this 'iconic' record (routinely described as his best work and/or the best album of the 1980s, even as one of the best albums of all time) might

---

8   Not to be confused, presumably, with the Seventh-day
     Adventist magazine *Signs of the Times*.

start with the fact that, in retrospect, it doesn't really hang together very well. Some of it is insanely good, but the mood is all over the place, and some of the sequencing is just plain messy. The dark cloud of the title track fades into the zippy, bubble-headed 'Play in the Sunshine', like a cheerfully inane TV announcer who cuts into the final minutes of *Apocalypse Now* with a *Wacky Races* cartoon. I can't be the only Prince fan whose ideal re-ordering of *Sign o' the Times* would start with the title-track and end with 'The Cross': from apocalypse to revelation. Instead, after the stark, theologically minded 'The Cross', for no good reason we leap into the so-so live track 'It's Gonna Be a Beautiful Night'. But a lot can be forgiven for the astonishing 'If I Was Your Girlfriend', in which Prince manipulates his voice into a creamy, anti-macho croon, not a definitively 'male' or 'female' voice but something beguilingly in between: a carnal angel.

This was the moment when Prince became fascinated by the 'ghost hardware' of remix, speeding his voice up or slowing it down into a series of phantom selves, in and out of a kind of plastic androgyny[9]. In comparison with all the future shock experimentation of tracks like 'Boyfriend', 'It' and 'The Ballad of Dorothy Parker', I never really quite bought the title song. I got the feeling it was less a banner of heartfelt protest than a bet Prince

9   His 'female' self – who at one point had a whole LP recorded and ready to go – he named Camille, apparently inspired by nineteenth-century French intersex person Herculine Barbin, who used the same alias. Michel Foucault, no less, rediscovered Barbin's memoirs in the 1970s while researching *History of Sexuality*, and had them republished; an English translation appeared in 1980. This baroque reference may have originated with Susannah Melvoin, as the workaholic Prince never seemed especially bookish.

had made with himself to see if he could do a perfect version of a certain 'type' of track – all those classic 1970s protest songs by the O'Jays, Curtis Mayfield, Stevie Wonder; lines like 'we're still putting people on the moon' and references to 'doing horse' sure don't sound much like 1987. Some people love the fact that *Sign o' the Times* collects every type of Prince song possible in one place, but to me it sounds like something patched together in a rush, with no real connecting membrane. And it remains an article of faith among hardcore fans that *Sign o' the Times* is indeed a pale shadow of his previous attempts to collate some or all of this mind-bending surplus material: the three unofficial albums known as *Camille*, *Crystal Ball* and *Dream Factory*.

8.
Here we run up against a problem. At this point, Prince decided things had gotten way too fancy, too playful, too... white. He needed to get back to his 'real' – which is to say his black – audience. Under this self-imposed fiat, he recorded something called *The Black Album*. He then withdrew it a week before it was scheduled for release, claiming it was in some way jinxed or haunted or evil, or something. The more prosaic truth may be that he suddenly realized how shockingly dull and pro-forma it sounded in comparison to his best work. All we really know is that sometime in 1987 Prince either finally fell apart, exhausted, or had some kind of semi-psychotic break, abetted by drugs he wasn't used to, or by breaking up with Susannah Melvoin, or by burrowing too far into a self-created mythology of Good Prince v. Bad Prince.

Yet what ultimately emerged from this mysterious episode was one of his most fascinating song suites, and his last great work: *Lovesexy* (1988), improbable as it sounds, is Prince's very own gospel album. On the sleeve he poses naked before God, as natural as the flowers that surround him. His lovesexy body looks lighter-skinned than earlier Princes, more like a Bollywood poster's supranational kitsch. Around his head is a nimbus of purple petals, and a distinctly phallic pistil inclines towards his chest, where his hand spreads to hide a crucifix from our worldly gaze. The lyrics swing between gnostic-sex nuttiness and determinedly naive stuff that could have been written for an adult version of *Sesame Street* – and something else too, something far more unnerving, something like Prince's showdown with his inner devil or Freudian death drive, which he gave the name 'Spooky Electric'.

If *Dirty Mind* was a hardcore celebration of the id, *Lovesexy* is less sure about the value of unapologetic 'badness'. Here he's debating the voices in his head: *'How dirty am I? Isn't dirty good? And if not, why not?'* Prince had made a career off his image as a steamy lover boy, yet now here he is at this relatively late stage, talking about a disabling hole in his life that can only be filled by 'learning to love ... the right way'. Some of the songs feel as if they've been worked on from the inside out, so that all their weird subtext is forced up front: 'No way to differentiate/between white and black/night and day.' The opening track, 'Eye No', seems on the face of it a big smiley hallelujah, but there's already a chill in the air. At one point, apropos of nothing, he whispers: 'The reason my voice is so clear/is there's no smack in my brain,' thus answering a question no one had asked. (Not that his voice is even that clear, as it happens.) The closing track is called 'Positivity', but the tone is distinctly edgy, downbeat, strung out: 'Don't kiss the beast, be superior at least... Hold on to your soul!' *Lovesexy* suggests a whole other world of 'spooky electric' sound, a kind of disembodied soul music from someone whose body has rebelled against him, which, sadly, he was never to explore further.

9.

In recovery from his spooky electric shock, Prince became obsessed with a certain idea of complete control. This turned out to be a disaster for his creative (and business) life: he continued to write and record songs at an inhuman rate, but the heart was AWOL, the spark gone. On *Diamonds and Pearls* (1991), he was in slickly professional hit-making form, but a lot of fans were left feeling queasy. The one genuinely heart-stopping song – the lovely, wistful 'Money Don't Matter Tonight' – is followed by the boilerplate funk of 'Push', which, bad as it is, isn't nearly as bad as 'Jughead'. There's an emptiness here which the painfully amped-up production cannot disguise. For all its sometimes heavy-handed sonics, *Diamonds and Pearls* is Prince Lite, assembled by a new cast of anonymous musicians, perfectly adequate professionals who would never surprise him (or us), and weren't in any position, as the now exiled Revolution had been, to demand their part in a genuine collaboration.

Is it just a coincidence that during his 1980s 'gnostic' phase his music was such an unpredictable delight, but that later, the more he takes on the promptings of a sterner, more dogmatic God, the music became more linear and formulaic? Back in 1985, during his first big Q&A on MTV, Prince said: 'I listened to all kinds of music when I was young ... I always said that one day I was gonna play all kinds of music and not be judged for the colour of my skin, but the quality of my work.' But now he seems to have decided what he wanted was an end to all giddy transmutation, and a return to something more real. Or at least, 'more real' in a millionaire muso-celebrity sense. This translated as a return to a black audience he claimed to have alienated with all his recent, artier departures. Which already sounded a tiny bit condescending, even before his new 'black' vision arrived, and it turned out to be a schoolboy caricature of shiny jewellery, fast cars, and scantily clad models. If everything up to this point felt like racial politics through a crazy looking glass, from hereon in things got a bit predictable: *real is black and black is real and it can never be anything else*.

The very thing that many of us thought was Prince's greatest achievement – that he became one of the biggest mainstream stars of his day without hiding or diluting his blackness, producing instead something you couldn't confidently call black *or* white – was now ditched in favour of songs with titles like 'Pussy Control': 'I want to hip y'all/to the reason I'm known as the playa of the year.' Prince trying to act 'gangsta' felt not merely silly and self-defeating, but almost a form of betrayal. Who ever said we looked to him for something 'real' or 'authentic', anyway? (Plus: two dozen prison-tat-sporting young rappers could do that stuff better in their sleep.) Oddly, at the same time he claimed to be returning to realer than real blackness, you'd swear he got two or three shades lighter for his publicity shots. In the group shot for *Musicology* (2004), he is the whitest-looking person in the seven-strong line-up – and that includes the white people. Or study the photo included in Draper's book of Prince playing with his protégée Tamar on *Good Morning, America* in 2006. She: full-on, in-your-face black woman. He: so pale he makes Stan Laurel look like Muddy Waters. Who knows what kind of Skin Game was being played (or replayed) here.

Prince claimed to hate revisiting his old songs, yet the music he now preferred to play was the stuff that seemed stuck in the past, while his music from the 1980s sounded more like the future than ever. On his website he was boasting of brave new technological innovations, but in his music he had retreated to a safe and homely funk. A song like 'My Name Is Prince' is the sort of ego-bomb manifesto most artists do early on, when they are still young enough that insane arrogance can seem cute and apt and winning. A middle-aged man desperately screaming that he's the one and only doesn't sound nearly so sweet. On the contrary, such macho theatrics may have a Trumpish effect: the more you insist on your uniqueness and invulnerability, the more it sounds like you're struggling. By the end of the track, he is simply repeating 'My name is Prince' over and over, going on for so long you begin to worry for his sanity. Perhaps the trouble was all those muscly young rapper dudes at his heels: 'My Name Is Prince' makes more sense once we imagine Prince howling that boast at *himself*, geeing himself up in a world that's changing fast.

Once, Prince had danced between identities; now it sounded like he was clinging to the side of an icy mountain in a force-ten gale, using his brand-name as a crampon. Granted, 'My Name Is Prince' comes out of an old-school black tradition, a James Brown style boast: 'On the seventh day he made – me!' But the tone is all wrong: there's no hint of send-up here, he sounds genuinely desperate rather than knowingly despotic. On the lamentable rap 'Sexy MF', there's no actual emotion in his voice; it's about as erotic as the cranked-up sound system in a tatty pole-dancing club – the tone is somewhere between resentful come-on and barely suppressed boredom. It's as if he had issued a proclamation: from now on you will enjoy my music in just one way – black and therefore pro forma funky. The Prince who once afforded glimpses of so many impossible futures had retreated into imoovable Tradition, making music that had only one origin, one destination, one reading – music like a recycled version of an old, old religion, no room left for any outsider's fresh interpolations.

10.
One evening recently I was in a local supermarket, which always has a surprisingly tasteful collection of old pop and soul hits as its background muzak. 'Raspberry Beret' came on and I just couldn't help it: I was instantly transported, singing along and showing out, right there in Aisle 3. It still sounded *so* good: those unexpected violins, the slightly 'off' backing vocals (a white girl sound, reversing the usual formula where a so-so white male lead is vamped by phenomenally good black female singers), the down-home cornbread of the song's narrative queered by tiny splinters of subtext that black listeners would immediately flash on (the singer's store-owning boss 'didn't like my kind/cuz I was way too leisurely...'). Was there really ever such a phantasmagorically odd pop hit as this, or was it all just a dream?

Following Prince's death in April 2016, a lot of people went online to write about what he had meant to them, remembering how hot and otherworldly he was in his pomp. Only, you couldn't help thinking they were grieving for someone who was, if not long gone already, then in truth long absent from the centre of anyone's thoughts. It had been so long since his music was everything it could be. In a song on *Emancipation*, from 1996, at which time he had renounced his name in favour of the symbol ⚥ Symbol-Prince sings a song about plain old Prince-Prince, and declares him 'dead as Elvis'. Most boys grow up with some kind of childish ambition to be king of this or that world, but what happens when a child is baptized Prince before he's said or done a thing? Right from the start of his career, names and naming, signs and alphabets, seemed to matter deeply to Prince. But what is a name, when you get down to it? It isn't something you can hold squarely in your hand like a lump of gold. It's wholly immaterial. It can make you feel like a god before your time – but equally, maybe, a ghost in your own life.

11.

The PP of Paisley Park's initials might also stand for Pleasure Principle – the idea that pleasure is the guiding principle of everything he dreams, and all he essays. Paisley Park was an imaginary space first (a microcosmic Eden, over the hills but very close by, where everyone was welcome: the halt, the lame, the uncool, the dorky, anyone whose beauty or sexuality didn't fit inside square society's miserly norms) before it became the name of Prince's Minneapolis-based complex, built with the profits from *Purple Rain*, comprising two recording studios, a dance studio, and a huge soundstage. It also contained living quarters and business centre. While it was undoubtedly a smart move on every level to have his own studio, you have to wonder, in retrospect, about the dangers of having everything he needed in one place. It's a kind of *Boy's Own* dream, this – with obvious dangers of insularity, of creeping alienation from the currents of life elsewhere, sealed off inside a hygienic smiley-face concept-world. He constructs a world in which absolutely nothing is left to chance; in which everything he sees, all around him, every hour of every day, is a reflection of no one and nothing but Prince. By the time of sets like 2006's *3121* we're all on the outside again, looking jealously in, our noses pressed against the glass of Prince's ultra-tasteful pad, his non-stop party, his supercool Hollywood pals. What was once a dream of happier community (sometimes black, sometimes an alchemical merger of all our colours) is now the same old story: I got mine, brother, screw you. Some fans insist *3121* is a high-minded biblical allegory, but I'm not buying it. (We put up with this kind of thing for decades from Prince: every time he came out with a new spiritual paradigm he shifted the goalposts, changed the rap, gave out a new party line which was short on convincing detail but long on wishy-washy utopian shine.) The combination of *Elle Decoration*-style shots of his Los Angeles rental and a front-of-sleeve shot of Prince, face to the wall with the titular number painted on his back, makes him look as if he's his own jailer in a luxury house-arrest. The Paisley Park pleasure principle ('The smile on their face/speaks of profound inner peace') has become a three-line whip promoting 24/7 hedonism. Prince is playing at Prince's house: music by Prince, décor by Prince, health-food snacks chosen by Prince. (I swear: he even installed a swear jar at Paisley Park.) There isn't a moment in the day, and not a detail anywhere – scent, serviette ring, artisanal stationery – in which he doesn't have the final say. Here is a small, deflating glimpse of what it may have been like being married to Prince: absolutely everything, including even your own pleasure, is conceived, conducted and monitored according to His royal tenets.

12.

Mayte Garcia's *The Most Beautiful: My Life With Prince* is the nearest thing we have to a believable portrait of private-life Prince. Even here, he glows distantly like a quasar, and it's hard to make out the lineaments of anything like a true inner life. There is something of a hummingbird effect: he keeps so busy you can't see through the blur to make any sense of why he behaves in the ways he does, or makes the decisions he does. A workaholic who writes endless songs about how much he supposedly enjoys just hanging out. A perfectionist who releases way too much substandard work. Garcia catalogues certain habits, tics, obsessions – yet we never really get a sense of Prince as a fully human presence, and the reason seems to be that she never did, either. 'As his wife, I could get closer than a girlfriend but ... there was a point of Do Not Enter.'

As with Madonna, there's the feeling that maybe no marriage could ever compete with the superstar's restless, near inhuman will-to-conquer. Far from using the book to get her own back, Garcia may even be underplaying her late husband's more infuriating behaviour, but nonetheless she reveals more about Prince than many fans will want to know, not least about his courtship of the 16-year-old Garcia. According to her, this was protracted but entirely innocent: no carnal border crossings until she was of legal age. Still, it's a fine line. Prince, she says, 'never denied the occasional impure thought crossed his mind, but the truth is, he was too wise and decent to take advantage of a 16-year-old'. By the end of *My Life with Prince* you may think that rather than being 'too ... decent to take advantage', he might have been sleazily wise enough to know that not taking advantage too soon was all part of a successful long-term grooming campaign. (At this point, I recall the strange voice, distorted and slowed to a devilish basso profundo, that opens *1999*: 'Don't worry – I won't hurt you – I only want you to have some fun.')

In general, Prince only had eyes for (much) younger women. 'I think his preference was more than physical,' Garcia writes. 'It was about the power balance. He didn't like to be argued with.' She quotes some of his love letters, written in his trademark semi-hieroglyphic number-pun alphabet. Again, this feels a tiny bit off, coming from a near-middle-aged roué: 'EYE'm glad U're young cuz U can wait 4 me.' Is this what it really means to be a 4-real beautiful dreamer – this state of arrested adolescence? Did he write this way to all his money men and lawyers, too? And what about the memoir ('The Beautiful Ones') he was said to be working on before his death: would that also have been set entirely in Prince-text?

Later, once they are married, Prince throws a huge strop when Garcia's father takes a happy snap of the happy couple. NOT ALLOWED, NO EXCEPTIONS: there are to be no unrehearsed photos anywhere in Paisley Park without prior arrangement. At which point, Prince's touchiness about image feels less like showbiz corn and something nearer undiagnosed pathology. You have the impression of someone who rarely, if ever, came out of character: there is no other side to this mirror. As with his heroes, James Brown and Miles Davis, it's hard to picture Prince outside a certain rigorously maintained 'look'. Black showbiz maintains a tradition not unlike that of European royalty, in which you always present yourself to your public in character and at your very best. Which is understandable, even laudable, but also something that might easily become unhealthy; not to mention a rather convenient excuse when someone closer to you than a worldwide audience demands a little more of the real you than you are prepared to give.

One of Garcia's frothier insights concerns someone known in Paisley circles as the 'foo foo master'. Whenever Prince toured, every hotel room he stayed in would be completely made over by this employee to exact, and exacting, Princely specifications: posh candles, fluffy rugs, general New Age... foof. (Prince even got into the habit of demanding a white baby grand piano for every hotel stop, until saner organizational minds prevailed.) Look in this mirror, children: each and every space is simultaneously fantastical, but also an endless repetition of the Same. Nothing ever changes in Prince World. Maybe on some level this was actually his ultimate fantasy? As if you were given a benevolent genie's wish and your answer was: 'O please let me have the exact same dream every single night!' Everywhere is home, nowhere is home.[10]

The most revealing part of Garcia's book concerns the birth and death six days later in 1996 of the child she calls Amiir (sometimes referred to elsewhere as Boy Gregory); he was born with Pfeiffer syndrome type 2, a rare genetic defect that causes the foetus's cranial bones to fuse, resulting in severe skeletal and systemic abnormalities. Garcia's account of the bizarre behaviour

10   In an interesting 2018 *New Yorker* article, 'Prince's Lonely Palace', Amanda Petrusich takes the official tour of Paisley Park and finds it a fairly gloomy and charmless experience. The impression one gets is that the Prince Estate is, not surprisingly, set on commemorating the pre-drug Prince, in all his colourful eccentricity; as if his death, and all that led to it, were just a tiny meaningless hiccup.

of her husband in the aftermath of the child's death is chilling. Maybe he retreated into a murky inner space because he was suffering in a way he had never learned to express; or because he knew himself well enough to know he had a void where such feeling should be. But it's more likely that in the absence of the usual human reflexes, he had installed an alternative set of wholly superficial showbiz habits, all emotion conceived in terms of what is or isn't made available for public consumption. Did he think it unmanly to be seen as in any way vulnerable? Did he find it impossible to unbuckle the rigid armour of his persona and admit that his rosy-fleshed mythos, equal parts happy carnality and religious utopianism, could end like this: with an 'imperfect' child, with medical disaster, death and grief?

Rather than seek privacy and cancel a scheduled appearance on Oprah, Prince seems to have entered a fugue state. He could surely have withdrawn, or maybe done the show alone, without Garcia. That instead he practically forces her, still unwell, still devastated, to stand in the glare of the TV lights and pretend everything is lovely in their marital garden seems cruel, oblivious, or demented. In answer to Oprah's gentle questioning about the child, Prince rolls out some pseudo-religious gobbledegook signifying that everything is absolutely right and joyful and as it should be, according to God's will. 'It's all good, never mind what you hear.' (By this point, the child was already dead, already ashes.)

Soon afterwards, Prince decides to go ahead with the promo for a new single ('Betcha By Golly Wow'), and says he wants the video to feature a sweetly ambiguous storyline mirroring the pregnancy, full of smiling children and twirling dancers and Mayte herself 'sitting on an exam-room gurney in [her] hospital gown'. Unbelievably, Prince asks her to do these scenes in the same room, in the same hospital she had only just left behind. Throughout the pregnancy, Garcia and Prince had argued about her medical treatment. As the wife of a multi-millionaire celebrity, she expected the very best obstetric care money could buy. Prince insisted that such diabolical science went against God's will, and that as a mere wife, she should unthinkingly go along with her husband's every command. Even when it became clear something wasn't right, Prince held fast. 'If there's something wrong,' he tells Garcia and the obstetrician, 'it's God's will. Not because we didn't prepare.' Later, after the birth, when the obstetrician tells him that Garcia must be checked back into hospital to allay the risk of permanent infertility, his immediate response, without consulting his wife, is: 'No. God's hand is on her. She'll be fine.'

We never do find out how Prince squared the fact that it all ended in such protracted agony for everyone involved, with his unshakeable faith in a God who always has everyone's best interests at heart. On the evidence of *My Life With Prince*, Garcia is someone almost supernaturally lacking in shade; the only passages where you feel she might be biting her tongue involve Prince's friend, Larry Graham. Graham, a funk bassist and 1970s soul star, was the man who brought Prince in to the Jehovah's Witness fold; there also seems to have been much manly midnight talk of the deep conspiracy stripe, the sort of 'revelations' that invariably involve numerology, acrostics, and brand name acronyms turned inside out to reveal their True Diabolical Meaning. In one song from *The Rainbow Children*, Prince notes portentously that 'the opposite of NATO is OTAN!' (Huh? Did he mean

Odin? Onan? Dano from *Hawaii Five-0*?)

As Garcia struggled to deal with a 'grief as airless and dark as the bottom of the ocean', Prince told her 'I can't be here, I have to go', and 'went to play a few gigs and promote the *Emancipation* album'. Where did Prince's own grief go? In the years following the loss of Amiir he released some of his all-time weakest work, on albums like *The Vault: Old Friends 4 Sale* and *Rave Un2 the Joy Fantastic*. Did the death of this child shut something down inside the adult Prince for good? You can only wonder what the rest of his life might have been like if things had turned out differently: if he had been completely open about this death so close to his own flesh; or if he'd been forced to take on the real life role of paternity, so long pictured as something purely symbolic. After his divorce from Mayte Garcia, in 2000, Prince got married again, on New Year's Eve 2001, to Manuela Testolini; she was 18 years younger than him and it appears he had already been seeing her while still married to Garcia. His second marriage lasted five years and there were no children.

13.

At the same time as Symbol-Prince was using Emancipation as his latest buzz word and preaching the gospel of The Rainbow Children, he suddenly found himself getting into trouble with a media that was no longer quite so worshipful or compliant. Example: claiming that women who had no choice about the burqa in Islamic countries 'were happy with that'. (His basic socio-politico line seems to have been: Let's face it, some people will always find *something* to moan about.) Then in 2008, when he was asked about his perspective on issues like gay marriage and abortion, Prince tapped his now ever present Bible and said: 'God came to the earth and he saw people sticking it wherever and doing whatever, and he just cleared it out. He was like, "Enough."' The man who would once have been the prophet of polymorphous perversity now reverted to a fall-back paradigm, as per Jehovah's Witness tenets, of old-fashioned marriage between Man and Woman. Ben Greenman: 'Prince repeatedly reiterated the presence of a "theocratic order," which expressly lays out the chain of command: God over man, man over woman.' There was also the matter of some 'theological' ideas that many observers found borderline anti-semitic. Greenman, again: 'His concept of the devil was especially problematic here. The lyrics weren't afraid to name names – and the names were Rosenblum, Pearlman and Goldstruck.'

You begin to wonder if his eventual adoption of the Jehovah's Witness faith was responsible for certain changes in his persona and personality; or whether he chose it precisely because it was such a serendipitous fit with the way he already felt about a fast-changing world, and how best to secure his own place within it.

Some fans might question the relevance any of this (plus some of the more personal revelations in Garcia's memoir) has to Prince's actual music; some may even bitterly grouse about there being way too few black faces in American public life as it is, and here's one more black man being taken down when he puts his head above the parapet. There might be something to argue in such objections, if it wasn't for the fact of certain undeniable patterns in the last decades of Prince's life. There were no isolated problems – when things went wrong, they fell away in droves, and in parallel. His need for absolute control in his private/business lives is mirrored by a similar need to patrol all avenues of meaning in his work: the minute he decided he was going to be just one kind of black artist playing one kind of black music, something curdled in his art; it lost a dimension or two. It was now perfectly smooth, funky, self-assured – and perfectly facile. He insists on party-time hedonism as if it were a biblical proscription; and he flings out biblical proscriptions as if they were showers of confetti meant to fall everywhere but his own shoulders.

14.
'There are necessary poisons, and some are extremely subtle, composed of ingredients from the soul, herbs collected from among the ruins of dreams, black poppies found next to the graves of our intentions...'
— Fernando Pessoa

Before April 2016, Prince wouldn't have been on anyone's list of showbiz people most likely to die of a drug overdose. We now know there had been problems for far longer than anyone suspected or wanted to admit. Garcia says there were 'several occasions when he told me he was "sick" or that he had a "migraine". Looking back I can see that it was something else.' In 1996, shortly after they lost their child, she surprised him on the *Emancipation* tour and 'found wine spilled on the rug in the hallway and vomit on the bathroom floor'. The Vicodin she had been prescribed for post-birth complications 'kept disappearing. The prescription would be filled, and a few days later, most of the pills would be gone. I assumed he was hiding them to keep me from hurting myself.' Prince evidently did a good job of bamboozling everyone around him; keeping the smiley mask polished bright had been second nature for a very long time. His studio 'vault' contained so many spare songs he could probably have continued for years without having to write anything new. When a song from 2006 boasts that his hot new funk is so on-trend it's coming down 'like the wall of Berlin, y'all!', you really have to wonder.

People can have an on-again off-again relationship with their drug of choice for years before fetching up with a full-blown addiction. Prince seems to have compressed this untidy, protracted arc just as his hero James Brown did, leaping overnight from disciplined abstinence to shivery chemical bondage. Never mind the occasional cheeky puff on a joint or weekend Ecstasy tumble: he goes straight to super-strength prescription narcotics. The official version is that it all began with operations Prince underwent on his poor shattered hips, frail after decades of on-stage athletics in unsuitable high-heels. An official investigation after his death by the authorities in Minneapolis revealed a situation that had gone way beyond any kind of measured therapeutics or sensible daily regimen: he was hip-deep in the sort of drugs normally administered only for extreme pain: the slivered no-self of atrocity survivors, or late-stage cancer patients. Garcia reports one of his long-time road crew confessing to her: 'Everything was great until *Purple Rain*. Then he got everything he ever wanted, and he didn't like it.' All that leftover time to fill! (I suddenly recall a phrase I used in the *NME*, in 1985 or thereabouts, when I – approvingly, at the time – described Prince and Michael Jackson as figures who had 'died into music'.)

In the final years of his life, Prince presented himself to everyone as a fulfilled and deeply religious man; but in private something was eating away at him. He was still rich, still handsome, sexually attractive, feted by younger musicians, still sold out concert halls around the globe. We should all have such mid-life crises! But how we feel about ageing is never simple, and anyone who lives long enough is eventually presented with a bill. Once again, it's hard not to feel there's some other story here, hiding behind the official version. In retrospect it seems less of a surprise, his embrace of those drugs, so much stronger in exact ratio to how much armour he needed to dissolve. Not just physical pain, but inner desolation, something that had gone untreated for a very long time. He'd been the unmoving spider inside his own web of absolute control for so long – how much of a relief must it have been to finally dive down into the oceanic bliss of his fearsome twenty-first-century opium?

15.

Prince's most affecting love song is a kind of phantom love letter, addressed to some lost or jettisoned part of himself. He never again produced anything remotely similar to 'Sometimes It Snows in April', the closing track on *Parade*: an otherworldly chiaroscuro of liquid acoustic guitar, piano caress and semi-wordless vocalese. Some of the lines are awkwardly sung-spoken, as if they had just popped into his head and he is squeezing them into the rhyme scheme, starting impossibly high then falling into a near-mumble, speeding up, slowing down, words on the edge of a meaning so personal it's hard to parse. One moment the singer is crying ('I used to cry for Tracy because he was my only friend...'), the next he is claiming 'No one could cry the way my Tracy cried', as if the singer himself were Tracy.

Maybe I'm just slow, or was hypnotized by the song's glacial beauty, but it was years before I realized what was going on in this dark and wistful snowsong, with its doubling, mirror-on-mirror effect. In the film *Under the Cherry Moon* (1986), for which *Parade* is putatively the soundtrack, this character fated to die, Christopher Tracy, is played by ... Prince. So, in effect, he's singing as someone else, and mourning his own introjected death. 'April' is Prince's love song to the split inside himself: the blithe, gigolo part has to die, in order to reclaim the traces of some other 'I' long-starved of attention. The song stops suddenly, unexpectedly: a tiny parallel death. (I knew quite a few people who turned to this song when friends or lovers were lost to AIDS in the 1980s/90s.) Turn the record over, back to the beginning, and we are back to the rush and bustle of 'Christopher Tracy's Parade', in which the titular Christ/opher is raised again, reborn.

It's the one Prince song that might fit comfortably in the catalogue of his long-term muse, Joni Mitchell. You can easily imagine mid-1970s Joni using the line 'a long-fought civil war' to describe some wounding amour. On 16 April 2016, five days before his death, Prince stopped off at a local record store and bought new copies of Stevie Wonder's *Talking Book* (1972) and Mitchell's *Hejira* (1976). Here was a past he felt comfortable with, also perhaps a clue to his ideal self: something halfway between funk-soul brotherhood and a pale, distant siren. *Hejira*: like *Parade*, another black and white sleeve, another blank-faced self-portrait. Icy light, dim faraway shadows; a black crow flying in a blue sky. Open up the gatefold and there is Joni, just like Prince and his mirror, viewed from behind and turning away: a dark-feathered bird of ill omen.

16.
'The precursor of the mirror is the mother's face.'
— D. W. Winnicott

Just before his death, Prince was playing all the old songs again: just himself, a piano and a microphone.[11] Playing the songs his fans wanted to hear, with appropriate lightness or gravity. People I know who saw these shows said they were something else: piercing, alive, unforgettable. And while it may not have been a meaningful solution to his long-term creative problems, maybe revisiting the emotions buried in those songs might have helped jog loose something inside. A breath of genuine memory, thoughts suitable for the age he was and not the silly, death-denying pretence of his Everywhere All the Time Party. Think of something like Mitchell's collection *Both Sides Now* (2000): a mixture of torch songs, old standards, new takes on such early classics as the title song and 'A Case of You'. She returns to these songs of her (and our) youth and sings them inside out, sings them with her 57-year-old voice and all it contains: all the love, desire, and disappointment; all the changes, choruses and chords; all the lessons learned from long hours working with brushes and paint. Cigarette smoke, lipstick and holy wine. A late Rembrandt self-portrait in song – and it's absolutely sublime.

He died alone, of course, in the middle of the night, between floors at Paisley Park, a heartbeat away from his studio. The middle of the night, when names and colours matter least. In the end, a painful reality triumphed over all easeful fantasy, and pain-numbing

11 *Piano and a Microphone 1983*, released in 2018 by Warner Brothers, is the name of the first set of original recordings to emerge from the Vault at Paisley Park since Prince's death.

drugs emptied out the interfering dialogue of every-one and everything else. One morning you awake and all the time has melted away: no more hotel bedroom afternoons, light moving like seaweed over the pale im-personal walls. All your life, dreaming of the other side of the mirror, where the colours all reverse, and now you finally remember what it was you saw in that dress-ing room mirror, so long ago: clouds, full of rain.

Bibliography

INTRODUCTION
Rythm oil, Stanley Booth
The Eggman and the Fairies: Irish Essays, Hubert Butler, John Banville (ed.)
The Invader Wore Slippers: European Essays, Hubert Butler, John Banville (ed.)
I'd Rather Be the Devil: Skip James and the Blues, Stephen Calt
Record Men: The Chess Brothers and the Birth of Rock and Roll, Rich Cohen
It Came from Memphis, Robert Gordon
Sweet Soul Music, Peter Guralnik
Twenty Thousand Roads: The Ballad of Gram Parsons and His Cosmic American Music, David N. Meyer
Under a Hoodoo Moon, Dr John (Mac Rebennack) with Jack Rummel
Where Dead Voices Gather, Nick Tosches
Escaping the Delta: Robert Johnson and the Invention of the Blues, Elijah Wald

EVEN IF YOU HAVE TO STARVE: THE LONG
HORIZONS OF MOD
Mod: A Very British Style, Richard Weight

DID HE FEEL GOOD? JAMES BROWN'S EPIC
LIFE AND CAREER
The One: The Life and Music of James Brown, R. J. Smith

BIRDITIS: THE OBSESSION WITH CHARLIE PARKER
Celebrating Bird: The Triumph of Charlie Parker, Gary Giddins
Kansas City Lightning: The Rise and Times of Charlie Parker, Stanley Crouch
Bird: The Life and Music of Charlie Parker, Chuck Haddix

THE FAST BIRTH AND SLOW OEDIPAL DEATH
OF ELVIS AARON PRESLEY
Elvis Has Left the Building: The Day the King Died, Dylan Jones
Elvis Presley: A Southern Life, Joel Williamson

HALF IN LOVE WITH BLIND JOE DEATH: GUITAR
VIRTUOSO JOHN FAHEY'S AMERICAN ODYSSEY
Dance of Death: The Life of John Fahey, Steve Lowenthal

SO HIP IT HURTS: STEELY DAN'S DONALD
FAGEN LOOKS BACK
Eminent Hipsters, Donald Fagen

THE QUESTION OF U: THE MIRROR IMAGE OF PRINCE

Prince: Life & Times, Jason Draper

The Most Beautiful: My Life With Prince, Mayte Garcia

Dig If You Will The Picture: Funk, Sex and God in the Music of Prince, Ben Greenman

Gold Experience: Following Prince in The 90s, Jim Walsh

Discography / Mood Map

INTRODUCTION
The Blues Volume 5, Various (Chess)
Dusty In Memphis, Dusty Springfield (Atlantic)
Total Destruction To Your Mind, Swamp Dogg (Alive)
In The Right Place, Dr John (Atlantic/Atco)
Ship Ahoy, O'Jays (Philadelphia International)
Trouble Man, Marvin Gaye (Motown)
The Gilded Palace of Sin, Flying Burrito Brothers (A&M)
They Say I'm Different, Betty Davis (Light In The Attic)
John Prine, John Prine (Atlantic)
Back To The World, Curtis Mayfield (Curtom/Charly)
Sweet Charlie Babe, Jackie Moore (Atlantic)
Caught Up, Millie Jackson (Southbound)
God Bless The Child, Billie Holiday (CBS)
Billie Holiday + Lester Young: A Musical Romance, Billy Holiday and Lester Young (Columbia/Legacy)
A Soldier's Sad Story: Vietnam Through the Eyes of Black America 1966-73, Various Artists (Kent)

EVEN IF YOU HAVE TO STARVE: THE LONG HORIZONS OF MOD
This Is Sue!, Various (Island Records LP)
Intensified! Original Ska 1962-1966, Various (Island Records LP)
Mose Allison Sings, Mose Allison (Prestige)
Italian Movie Soundtracks, Chet Baker (WaxTime LP)
My Generation, The Who (MCA)
Everybody Digs Bill Evans, Bill Evans Trio (DOL)

DID HE FEEL GOOD? JAMES BROWN'S EPIC LIFE AND CAREER
Soul Classics Vol II, James Brown (Polydor)
James Brown's Funky People (Part 2), James Brown (Polydor/Universal)
Funky Good Time: The Anthology, The J.B.s (Polydor/Chronicles)

BIRDITIS: THE OBSESSION WITH CHARLIE PARKER
Charlie Parker on Dial Volume 3, Charlie Parker (Spotlite)
Best of The Complete Savoy & Dial Studio Recordings, Various (Savoy)
West Coast Time, Charlie Parker (Charlie Parker Records)

SWOONATRA: THE AFTERLIVES OF FRANK SINATRA
Francis Albert Sinatra & Antonio Carlos Jobim: The Complete Reprise Recordings,
Frank Sinatra and Antonio Carlos Jobim (Universal)
Watertown, Frank Sinatra (Reprise)
20 Golden Greats, Frank Sinatra (Capitol)
Sinatra: London, Frank Sinatra (Universal)

THE FAST BIRTH AND SLOW OEDIPAL DEATH
OF ELVIS AARON PRESLEY
Elvis at Stax, Elvis Presley (RCA)

HALF IN LOVE WITH BLIND JOE DEATH: GUITAR
VIRTUOSO JOHN FAHEY'S AMERICAN ODYSSEY
The Contemporary Guitar Sampler, Various (Topic)
The Transfiguration of Blind Joe Death, John Fahey (Topic)
Return of The Repressed, John Fahey (Rhino)

SO HIP IT HURTS: STEELY DAN'S DONALD
FAGEN LOOKS BACK
The Okeh Ellington, Duke Ellington (Columbia)
Blues In Orbit, Duke Ellington (Columbia)
Jazz In The Space Age, George Russell & His Orchestra (Decca/
ChessMates/Universal)
The Music From Peter Gunn, Henry Mancini (RCA Victor)
Song For My Father, Horace Silver (Blue Note)
Can't Buy A Thrill, Steely Dan (MCA)
Pretzel Logic, Steely Dan (MCA)
The Nightfly, Donald Fagen (Warner Bros)

THE QUESTION OF U: THE MIRROR STAGE OF PRINCE
Parade, Prince (Paisley Park)
Piano & A Microphone 1983, Prince (NPG/Warner Bros)

Acknowledgements

All these pieces originally appeared in *City Journal* and the *London Review of Books*. (A happy accident, this cross-Atlantic pairing.) Working for both publications has been a notably agreeable experience – being treated like a human being and a seasoned professional and suitably rewarded for your labour shouldn't be such a surprising thing, but sadly, there it is. I'd like to thank Mary-Kay Wilmers, Paul Myerscough and Nick Richardson at the *LRB* for editorial care, collaboration, and patience beyond the call. I especially want to thank Brian C. Anderson at *City Journal*: at a time when I wasn't far off chucking it all in and re-training as a cat therapist, he got in touch out of the blue, with an offer I couldn't refuse. *City Journal* is the house magazine of an American conservative think-tank and is mainly read by – well, the sort of people who esteem the sort of viewpoints generated by an American conservative think tank. Brian opened his venerable pages to me (a defiantly old school socialist-hedonist) to write about, inter alia, James Brown, Joan Didion and Walter Benjamin; at a time when ideological point-scoring has descended so low that to use the word 'gutter' would be a kindness, this warms the heart, to say the least. Talking of things that warm the heart, I'd like also to thank Brian Dillon, for a precisely timed and very kind elbow to my ribs. Finally, as ever I owe a huge and ever-growing debt to Su Small, aka Mrs P, whose support continues to make everything possible. ('... and they all led me straight back home to you.')

These pages are dedicated to the memory of...
Geoff Rushton, aka John Balance
Mark Fisher, aka K-Punk
Gary Phillips, aka pixiejuniper
and my beautiful pawboy, Biggie.

Fitzcarraldo Editions
8-12 Creekside
London, SE8 3DX
United Kingdom

ISBN 978-1910695-87-6

Design by Ray O'Meara
Typeset in Fitzcarraldo
Printed and bound by TJ International

fitzcarraldoeditions.com

Fitzcarraldo Editions